THE HOUSE

THE HOUSE

INSIDE THE

ROYAL OPERA HOUSE

COVENT GARDEN

KATE MOSSE

'Music is well said to be the speech of angels'

Thomas Carlyle, 'The Opera', 1838

BBC BOOKS

This book is published to accompany the television series entitled
The House – Inside the Royal Opera House, Covent Garden.
The series was produced by Double Exposure.

EXECUTIVE PRODUCER (BBC) Edward Mirzoeff
SERIES PRODUCER Andrew Bethell
PRODUCER AND DIRECTOR Michael Waldman

Published by BBC Books,
an imprint of BBC Worldwide Publishing.
BBC Worldwide Limited, Woodlands,
80 Wood Lane, London W12 0TT

Designed by Harry Green
All black and white photographs by David Secombe
(excluding those on pages 120, 121 and 180)
Picture research by David Cottingham

Set in Bembo
Printed in Great Britain by Cambus Litho Ltd, East Kilbride
Bound in Great Britain by Hunter & Foulis Ltd, Edinburgh
Colour separations by Radstock Reproductions Ltd, Midsomer Norton
Jacket printed by Lawrence Allen Ltd, Weston-Super-Mare

FRONTISPIECE The familiar white Victorian building looking down on Bow Street
is the third theatre to have stood on the Covent Garden site since 1732.
The first playhouse, together with all the buildings around it, burned to the ground in 1808.
Its successor – the first centrally-heated theatre in Britain – followed suit in 1856.
E M Barry's distinctive Corinthian-columned theatre opened for business in 1858.
It was not until 1892 that it became known as the Royal Opera House.

C O N T E N T S

ACKNOWLEDGEMENTS
PAGE 6

OVERTURE
PAGE 8

SEPTEMBER 1993
PAGE 16

OCTOBER 1993
PAGE 23

NOVEMBER 1993
PAGE 42

DECEMBER 1993
PAGE 62

JANUARY 1994
PAGE 77

FEBRUARY 1994
PAGE 91

MARCH 1994
PAGE 105

APRIL 1994
PAGE 119

MAY 1994
PAGE 142

JUNE 1994
PAGE 150

JULY & AUGUST 1994
PAGE 162

FINALE
PAGE 177

LIST OF 1993/94 PRODUCTIONS
PAGE 187

INDEX
PAGE 189

ACKNOWLEDGEMENTS

This book is based on the six-part television series *The House – Inside The Royal Opera House, Covent Garden*, made by Double Exposure for BBC2. For nearly a year – September 1993 to August 1994 – BBC director Michael Waldman and his team shadowed everyone who worked in and around the Royal Opera House, Covent Garden. They, in their turn, were shadowed by me.

The aim was to create a living portrait of the institution itself, one of Britain's most enduring and loved lyric theatres. It would not be a bland snapshot, mere name-dropping of the world's greatest living exponents of opera and ballet. Instead, *The House – Inside The Royal Opera House, Covent Garden* was to be a series which would bring the hundreds of women and men behind the scenes into the spotlight, those stars behind the stars who make Covent Garden the place it is. The glittering productions, the celebrated faces, would be included too, but as part of a richer, more inclusive and unique, whole.

A prodigious patience and tenacity are required in fly-on-the-wall film-making. There is always the danger that those being filmed will perform rather than allow themselves to be watched. To a degree, the trick is not only to be in the right place at the right time with your camera running, but to recognize the right place when you find it. *A priori* judgements need to be challenged, replaced by a willingness to listen and watch and wait, just in case. Later, there is the ruthlessness essential if the many, many precious rolls of film are to be reduced to a few captivating hours of television, a coherent and thoughtful narrative.

What follows is the story of the 1993/94 Season at the Royal Opera House. It is not a chronological note-by-note account of every conversation as it happened, of every ballet and opera, so much as a personal broad-brushed interpretation of life at the House during one particular Season. Not everything could be squeezed in, so the space I have given to the work of the Education Department and The Birmingham Royal Ballet, for example, fails to do justice to their achievements. The spirit of the book comes from being inside the House itself – months spent front and backstage, the face-to-face interviews squashed in between meetings, rehearsals, performances – as well as my days with The Royal Ballet on tour and the weeks and weeks rooted in airless rooms at the offices of Double Exposure, jotting down notes as I watched 'rushes', the raw unedited sound and pictures from which a television series is built.

So, to the cast list. First, my thanks to all those at The Royal Opera House itself whose generosity and trust made the process of researching and writing the book so satisfying. Because it is a narrative, not an analytical index of productions and personnel, my apologies to those who feel left out or slighted at not being mentioned.

David Secombe was not only good company as we prowled backstage, but is a maestro amongst the rank-and-file photographers. He has a rare ability to capture the truth of people – personality, tension, drama, emotion – without being intrusive.

My thanks to everyone at Double Exposure who shared with me the process of making a documentary series: Andrew Bethell, Jean MacFarlane and Michael Waldman. Special thanks go to Researchers Laura Ashton for her good-humour and support and Max Carlish, for his stamina and enthusiasm – guiding me round the House itself and through the 'rushes'.

At BBC Worldwide Publishing, my thanks to Editorial Director Sheila Ableman and photo researcher David Cottingham. Having lived with a project for so long, the last few months of revising, editing, proof-reading can be painstaking, dispiriting even: the intelligence, energy and wit of my editor, Barbara Nash, made them fun.

At the Peters, Fraser and Dunlop Agency my gratitude goes to Mark Lucas. Despite his supernatural ability to ring at the very worst times of day or night, I am glad of his acuity and cheerful arm-twisting in persuading me to accept the commission in the first place.

Several friends came to the rescue in practical ways, offering quiet places to work or the use of a printer that could cope with foreign words: Astier Almedom and Alex de Waal, Jonathan and Rachel Dunk, Lucinda Montefiore, Robert Dye, Frances Rodgers and especially Jonathan Evans.

Finally, my family. Five-and-a-half-year-old Martha (who wants to be a ballerina) and Felix (who, at the age of three, does not) were less jealous of the word processor than might have been expected, especially as I was still playing with it rather than with them the day before Christmas ... And Greg. It is impossible to describe the depth of his love, support and pride without lapsing into words that are either clichéd or bland. Perhaps it is enough to say that without him and Martha and Felix there would be no point to any of this. It is to them that this book is dedicated.

'Never once in television, admittedly in its fat and happy days, did I not have adequate resources to do the job. Here, the process of trying to pay the bills goes on all year.'

Jeremy Isaacs, General Director

OVERTURE

The summer holidays were over. Jeremy Isaacs, General Director of the Royal Opera House, sat in his office. A car alarm pierced the quiet of the street below. In just over a week the 1993/94 Season would kick off, opera followed five weeks later by the ballet. And by the time the House closed for its summer break eleven months later, hundreds of thousands of people would have been dazzled by Mozart and Janáček, Rossini and Wagner, Verdi and Tchaikovsky.

It was an impressive, glittering line-up this year. Two of the three tenors were coming – Plácido Domingo and José Carreras – and Jeremy Isaacs himself had been instrumental in persuading Luciano Pavarotti back to Covent Garden the following Season, after a three-year absence. Some of the greatest sopranos would be in London, divas Dame Kiri Te Kanawa and Mirella Freni among them. Welsh bass-baritone Bryn Terfel, American mezzo Denyce Graves and Romanian soprano Angela Gheorghiu were names that might draw the autograph hunters in a few years time. The brilliant ex-Royal Shakespeare Company director, Trevor Nunn, had been persuaded to make his House directing opera début proper in March.

And The Royal Ballet Company, combining home-grown talent such as Darcey Bussell and Viviana Durante and international dancers with worldwide reputations – not least the notorious Sylvie Guillem from the Paris Opéra Ballet and ex-Bolshoi star Irek Mukhamedov. With a big American tour at Easter, this Season could turn out to be one of their most successful for years.

Seven new productions and thirteen revivals from The Royal Opera Company, four mixed programmes and four full-length ballets presented by The Royal Ballet, from *Aida* to *Tales of Beatrix Potter*, there was something for everyone. Here, surely, was a British cultural institution of which to be proud. And yet ...

In the Board Room the mood was more one of uncertainty and change than of triumph. Money was tight and getting tighter. Not only did the House have a £3.6 million deficit to shift, but relations between it and its primary sponsor – the Arts Council of Great Britain – were resentful and tetchy. A year earlier, Mary Warnock had produced a report on what the Arts Council considered to be the 'unprecedented crisis' at Covent Garden. The House had stood accused of weak management, of archaic industrial relations and a seeming inability to strike the right balance between artistic integrity and financial responsibility. Now, in September 1993, despite assurances of support – and notwithstanding the best fence-mending efforts of Sir Angus Stirling, Chairman of the Main Board – the Council was hinting that the Opera House might be faced with a two per cent cut to their £19 million annual subsidy.

Plus ça change, plus c'est la même chose. Back in 1952, the Chancellor of the Exchequer had been forced to approve a £50 000 one-off 'rescue-operation' for Covent Garden and, over the past twenty years, there had been a succession of reports into House finances: so much money spent on investigating how the money was spent.

For the Royal Opera House, as for so many others, forced conversion to the 1980s religion of market forces had been painful. However much the critics might cheer or boo particular productions, volleying attacks by a significant handful of journalists and politicians on the institution itself were common. To some it was a bastion of élitism, a monument to how tax payers' money was being used to finance the entertainment of a small band of very privileged, very arrogant people. Conveniently overlooking the fact that there were tickets costing less than the price of a seat in a West End cinema, opponents continued to lambast the less-than-frequent spectacle of £129 seats for Grand Opera in the Grand Tier.

The House was, in fact, in possession of a much lower subsidy than any comparable lyric theatre in Europe. But to detractors high prices were inexcusable in the face of such a high level of public funding and, in their opinion, a direct consequence of years of inefficiency and profligacy. When really down on its uppers, reminded the splenetic pens, The Royal Opera had spent several hundred pounds on one pair of scarlet thigh boots sported by baritone Thomas Allen in Mozart's *Don Giovanni*. What was that, if not a clear indication of the House's refusal to cut its artistic cloth according to his budget? (Those notorious boots were, in fact, now over ten years old, but were still trotted out as evidence for the prosecution of the wanton squandering of other people's money.)

None of this was new, of course. What was new was the level of uncertainty about the future of Covent Garden itself. It was no longer just a question of balancing the books or persuading the public that the Royal Opera House was worth every penny. Now major eleventh-hour decisions had to be taken about the actual building. Come what may, new European Union Health and Safety regulations would force the House to close for refurbishment in 1997. But for how long? And how extensive would the renovations be? As the new season kicked off in September 1993, speculation over the very existence of the Royal Opera House was adding a sharper edge to the newspaper coverage.

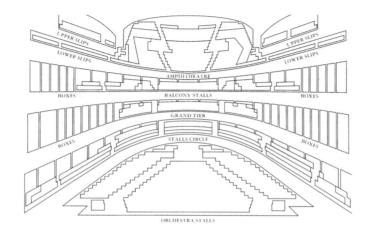

There are over 2000 seats in
the horse-shoe shaped Auditorium, from the Orchestra Stalls at ground level
to the Upper Slips at the very top corners of the House.

There has been a theatre on the Covent Garden site since 1732. In 1858, E. M. Barry's white-columned Victorian building rose out of the ashes of two earlier theatres destroyed by fire. In 1892 electricity had replaced gas, then ten years later the heavy stage machinery was installed. The building survived the two world wars intact – as a furniture repository during the First and a Mecca Palais de Danse for most of the Second – and remained untouched until 1964 when it was rewired and the Gallery and Amphitheatre reinforced. To all intents and purposes, the Victorian theatre – a Grade I listed building – had been by-passed by the twentieth century.

But for nearly twenty years there had been a transforming vision of a glittering, twenty-first century opera house in the heart of London. Paving the way for a major redevelopment, the island site on which the theatre stood – Russell Street to the south, Floral Street to the north, James Street to the west and Bow Street to the east – had been acquired in 1974 by the Labour Government and vested in the Royal Opera House Development Land Trust, with the House and the Arts Council as co-trustees. Three years later, the freehold of the building itself was bought and vested in the Royal Opera House Board.

Although not without its problems, Phase I of the redevelopment was finished in 1983 at the tail-end of the bicentennial celebrations. The existing building was extended up to James Street, with airy rehearsal facilities for the opera, spacious wardrobes and dressing rooms, each with its own piano and bathroom, and two ballet studios. Before that, ballet rehearsals had even been held in the Crush Bar. Nine years later, the ground floor and basement levels fronting James Street were turned into shops and restaurants.

But everyone knew that it was Phase II of the redevelopment which would make the difference and transform the Victorian building into a modern theatre to rival the Metropolitan Opera House in New York, the Bastille in Paris. The traditional horseshoe-shaped Auditorium meant that there were seats with semi-restricted or restricted views. Even though the basic shape would remain the same, the Auditorium would at least be bigger (85 more seats available). More seats would mean larger audiences and hopefully lower prices, that was the idea. They wanted to build a second Auditorium as well, a 300- to 500-seater to house education projects and perhaps even smaller touring companies.

There would be space behind the curtain, too: the cramped wings and Dickensian backstage area would become the stuff of memory. It was not just a question of creature-comforts for performers and stagehands – although that was one consideration – but more that the existing system was inefficient, unsafe and wasteful. The Stage machinery was powered by First World War submarine engines and it was high time they were decommissioned. The House wanted to install a sort of gigantic Rubik's cube system, much like the one in the new Opera House in Gothenburg, so that whole sets could be raised and lowered intact one after another: stagehands would not have to construct and dismantle heavy sets after every rehearsal, every performance, because of lack of storage space. Fewer people would be needed, the work would be less physically demanding, shows could be turned round more quickly. Afternoon rehearsals would become possible.

As on the Stage, so above it. With a fully-powered flying system, pieces of scenery and backcloths could be lowered and raised quickly and safely. No longer would there be a team of men (and one woman) in the Flies working on narrow galleys high above the Stage and Wings, loading and unloading lead weights on to antique rope pulley systems by hand.

When empty, there is an expectant hush in the Auditorium that makes you want to run your hand along the back of the seats. In the narrow Wings the air always feels just stilled, as if only recently abandoned by performers and technicians and flowers and orders: 'Fly cue 3, go; LX cue 41, go; stand by Fly cue 4'.

Here have stood Maria Callas and Tito Gobbi, Margot Fonteyn and Rudolf Nureyev. In the Pit, the batons of Beecham, Furtwängler, Mehta and Solti have inspired hundreds of oboists, cellists and percussionists.

Embracing the Stage, miles of indistinguishable narrow corridors randomly punctuated by swing doors, lead around and under and back again: you can smell the Canteen, but somehow you can't find it; the miracles of Make-Up are supposed to be just round this corner. As you search, bursts of tantalizing music escape over the tannoy system. Thousands of performers have found themselves wandering hopelessly lost in the corridors, these tales as much a part of the folklore of the Royal Opera House as the autographed photographs hanging on the walls.

This living tradition, handed down from one generation of artists to the next, is one of the things that gives the Royal Opera House its spirit of place. In the Wings, in the Auditorium and most especially on the Stage itself, it is this sense of being part of a celebrated history that draws performers again and again. In part – and despite the obvious drawbacks – this was precisely why the House wanted to stay where it was rather than be rehoused in a purpose-built theatre. 'It's the right decision for this peculiar British society which clings to its past,' said Jeremy Isaacs resolutely, beetle-browed. 'We deliver something to Britain that Britain needs.'

Rather than spend nearly two years and £25 million merely patching up the building, the Board vowed bullishly to champion its vision: the House would go dark at the end of the 1996/97 Season, reopening late in 1999 as a world-class opera house to welcome in the millennium. It would be a theatre for the future, grounded in the triumphs and traditions of the past. An elegant landmark, it would be an appropriate celebration of national artistic excellence and cultural identity.

Overall planning consent for the Phase II redevelopment had been granted in May 1990. However, since 1983, there had been strong opposition almost every step of the way, from the Covent Garden Community Association, from Westminster City Council and from the House's paymasters, the Arts Council. If London's lyric theatres were already struggling to fill the seats available every night – the evidence was that both ballet and, to a lesser degree, opera audiences were shrinking – then why provide more? Would the public benefit from the huge sums of money being spent on its behalf? Could there not be change without destroying the beautiful historic facades of buildings surrounding the Opera House? Many

'I'm a battler and I love it here, believe in what we're doing. But this is the hardest job I've ever done, by a street.' Jeremy Isaacs, General Director, contemplating the Dickensian working conditions backstage.

market-traders would lose their handed-down pitches if rehearsal facilities for the ballet replaced them as planned. Why? As this bad-tempered consultation process progressed in fits and starts, millions of pounds had been spent without another brick being laid.

And 1997 cruised ever closer. No home had yet been found for the orchestra, ballet or opera companies during the closure period. No job assurances had yet been given to the 1100-strong skilled workforce, only promises that assurances would be given. And, above all, no one had yet agreed to pay.

It was against this backdrop that Jeremy Isaacs and Sir Angus Stirling were allowing the BBC to film. 'We've decided to let them into the building,' he explained a couple of weeks later at a lunch for corporate and individual supporters. 'It is completely impossible for anyone to behave naturally in the presence of a camera and a microphone. But, now we have got used to the fact that whenever you think you're on your own, there they are, just behind you, we're rather enjoying having them here!'

With his distinctive pugnacious profile, Jeremy Isaacs is a disarming mixture of candour and bullishness. One of the biggest players in British television – Channel 4's founding Chief Executive and the best Director General the BBC never had – he is, in many ways, the ultimate outsider. His early years as General Director of the Royal Opera House had not been easy. With a superiority born of years of practice, some within the ranks of the organization itself had believed that Isaacs, a mere telly man, would need to be taught a thing or two about the performing arts and British culture. The assassination-by-newsprint brigade had deplored his bull-in-a-china-shop approach, pinpointing wrong decisions taken over-hastily. And a few had wondered at the wisdom of appointing this unorthodox man to one of the most traditional of British institutional roles. But Jeremy Isaacs is nothing if not a fighter and, bit by bit, his passion and determination to transform the Royal Opera House had won over many former critics. He is popular with the rank-and-file, too, a man who talks to everyone, who respects everyone's contribution, whether they be cleaners, stagehands or divas.

On several occasions over the past few years documentary film companies had approached the Royal Opera House with a view to capturing the backstage spirit of the place. All had been refused and the doors had remained closed to the prying eyes of the cameras. Jeremy Isaacs knew better than most that fly-on-the-wall series were a gamble. The possibilities for misrepresentation were endless, an ill-chosen word here, a grimace there when what was intended was a wry smile. But by September 1993, after five years at the helm, he felt that their combined efforts meant that the place was 'humming in the right sort of way'. Perhaps the time was right to let the world outside see just how much had changed, despite the impressions given by some scribblers to the contrary. BBC Director Michael Waldman and the Double Exposure team were allowed to start filming.

Behind Isaacs's and Stirling's decision was a wish to be understood. If only people knew exactly what was involved in running a theatre the size of Covent Garden, then perhaps the hard work, the commitment and the sheer virtuosity of the juggling acts being performed by everyone in the House, top to bottom, would be applauded rather than just criticized. Surely informed opinion, even if unfavourable, had to be better than 'glib, superficial, unknowing' – as Isaacs put it – column inches about value for money? 'I'm a battler and I love it here,' he added impatiently. 'I believe in what we're doing. But this is the hardest job I've ever done, by a street.'

'All series that purport to be giving an actual account of what is really going on in an institution are false, because what they are really showing is how people behave in front of cameras.' Jeremy Isaacs (left) with Nicholas Payne, Director of The Royal Opera, in the Auditorium.

'The other day my secretary told me sharply that I ought to be thinking about opera's future as an art form in the twenty-first century. I'm quite sure she's right, but most of the time in this job it's hard to think much further than next Thursday.'

Nicholas Payne, Director of The Royal Opera

SEPTEMBER

Saturday, 11 September 1993, six-thirty p.m. In half an hour the curtain would go up on Puccini's *Madama Butterfly*. Women in elegant dresses and men in smart jackets strolled across the cobbled stones of the Covent Garden piazza. The Amphitheatre audience snaked in from Floral Street. Around the corner, outside the main white-columned entrance in Bow Street, chauffeurs stationed their long cars. The doors opened and closed with barely a sound.

Inside the Crush Bar, people looked down on the elegant traffic jams in the street below. Here, those in some of the most exclusive, most expensive seats had come to drink and be seen. The sound of Champagne bottles in ice-buckets mingled with the bubbles of social questions about health, summer holidays, sons' A-level results, daughters' degrees. The air smelled rich, Givenchy and Chanel superimposed on the wisps of cigarette smoke. Peter Torini, one of the two barmen in the Crush Bar, juggled glasses, bottles, £20 notes. Customers, squeezed sideways along the bar, tried to catch his eye and place their orders for interval drinks.

'Originally I trained to be an opera singer,' confided Peter. 'I came here just to get some extra work while I studied. Unfortunately they were better than I was, so realism set in.' He controls the end of the Crush Bar furthest from the staircase.

'It's only the more knowledgeable who come up this end,' he said between pouring gins and tonics. 'I started at that end and worked my way along the bar. It took me thirty years to do it, but I did it eventually. It was like a scene from one of the operas, you know, I ascended the throne. This was always the better end of the bar because all the administrators come here – David Webster, John Tooley – and all the others. Isaacs has broken the pattern, he went down the other end ... '

The other end is Bill Griffin's territory. It is a war zone, a no-man's land in the middle separating the two commanders.

'Over the years, contempt has bred contempt,' said Peter. 'So he's down there and I'm up here and it's perfect. We don't speak, not at all for eighteen months. We just communicate if the phone rings, that's it.'

Perfectly modulated hubbub, a night out at the opera. In his long tail coat, red waistcoat and bow tie, Ivell Arnold, Commissionaire Manager, drew in his breath.

'Welcome to the Royal Opera House ladies and gentlemen. Will you now please enter the Auditorium. Thank you.' Glasses are drained, smokers search for somewhere to stub out. Directions are given, as hands fish in pockets and handbags for tickets.

'Hurry along now please, ladies and gentlemen, the lights are about to go down. Will you now please enter the Auditorium.'

There are a few last-minute dashes to the Ladies cloakroom in the vain hope that the queue will have shrunk. There is no queue in the Gents.

'Ladies and gentlemen, the performance is about to start. If you hurry, you will just make it ladies and gentlemen.'

The bell rings for the last time. The doors shut. Inside the Auditorium, the audience settles down to await Puccini's Pinkerton.

Most theatres in the West End are home to only one production at a time. Some shows – *Les Misérables*, say – run for years, others come and go. But the Royal Opera House is a repertory theatre. The two resident companies – The Royal Ballet and The Royal Opera – share the Stage for a fixed season, with performances by their sister company, The Birmingham Royal Ballet (also administered by the Royal Opera House), guest appearances by touring companies such as Opera North and one-off galas and festivals slotted in around them. So, every single day of the Season, sets are built and dismantled on Stage, with no time for slippage. Matinées, early kick-off evening performances, special schools matinées complete a full performance diary.

At first glance, the economics and logistics of mounting opera and classical ballet seem cock-eyed: huge sums of money for a tiny number of dates. The first new production of the 1993/94 Season – *Die Meistersinger von Nürnberg* – was programmed to open nearly a month after *Madama Butterfly*. With its huge cast and massive Wagnerian orchestra, it was an expensive opera to mount, budgeted to cost £350 000. There were only to be six performances,

In the Crush Bar Ivell Arnold clutches his
Commissionaire's Bible – which gives the running time, plot and cast for every performance –
as he prepares to usher in the audience. 'Welcome to the Royal Opera House, Ladies and Gentlemen.
Will you now please enter the Auditorium. Thank you.'

though, so by the time word of mouth reached many ordinary punters they found it was too late to buy a ticket.

But actually any new production – the sets, costumes, lighting, the novel artistic interpretation – is an investment for the future, not just for one Season. For example, Kenneth MacMillan's first professional ballet, *Danses concertantes*, has been in The Royal Ballet's repertoire since 1955.

Meistersinger would be added to The Royal Opera's repertoire so that the production could earn its keep over many, many years. For the House, it would be deemed a financial success in 1993 if the Auditorium was filled.

The trick is in scheduling a fast turnover of different sorts of productions. Not only does this give a financial safety-net if a controversial production proves unpopular – spreading the load, if you like – but it also means that audiences do not have to wait long for an opera or ballet more to their taste.

It is a competitive business, as the Director of each company haggles and negotiates for the productions he wants, for the budgets he thinks he needs and for enough Stage time to make the commitment and skill worthwhile. Both Directors must marry vibrancy and innovation with sure-fire crowd-pleasers, accepting that contemporary work is harder to sell than Mozart, Verdi or Tchaikovsky.

In one corner is Anthony Dowell – Director of The Royal Ballet – one of the most graceful and gifted British classical dancers of the twentieth century, and one half of the celebrated partnership with Antoinette Sibley. He joined the company in 1961, his beauty and elegance inspiring The Royal Ballet's two distinguished resident choreographers, Frederick Ashton and Kenneth MacMillan. Dowell became Norman Morrice's assistant in 1984, took over from him as Director two years later and is held in awe by many of the dancers. 'It's always a big thing when he comes into a rehearsal,' admitted Vanessa Palmer, a young First Artist in the Corps de Ballet. 'Everyone wants to prove themselves to him because of the great dancer he was.'

Popular and witty though Anthony Dowell is, he is not a natural member of paper-shuffling management. For him, there is a 'star wars' atmosphere when he is called to account to the Ballet Board, a bi-monthly ordeal of leaping through hoops within hoops. His Administrative Director, Anthony Russell-Roberts, temporized: 'They're intelligent people and they ask intelligent searching questions … but you can never tell which way they will jump'.

Like the three other subsidiary boards – for the Opera, for the Development and for The Birmingham Royal Ballet – the Ballet Board has to answer to the Main Board, where the final axe falls.

In the other corner is Nicholas Payne, Director of The Royal Opera. Having worked in the House's Finance Department for a couple of years in the late 1960s, he was appointed General Administrator of Opera North in 1982 after stints at the Arts Council and the Welsh National Opera. Dividing his time between Leeds and Covent Garden for the earlier part of the year, September 1993 was the beginning of his first full season in charge. And because opera seasons are planned three or so years ahead, he was mostly inheriting responsibility for other people's ideas.

Always late for meetings, always clutching his olive green mug of black coffee, Nicholas Payne is a skilful lobbyer with a healthy appetite for the honourable combat in which he has to engage with the Opera Board to get what he wants: 'Jeremy Isaacs and I have the executive power until we abuse it in such a way that they fire us. Even though it's not the Main Board, the Opera Board can have a lot of power if it uses its power cleverly'.

It is a sensitive issue allocating Stage time and money throughout the intensive forty-seven-week season. In the final analysis, though, the preferences of either company must be weighed against the financial, as well as artistic, needs of the House as a whole. As recently as five years ago ballet was more viable at the Box Office than opera, now opera has the upper hand: a Christmas present of a centre seat in Row A of the Balcony for an evening performance of Puccini's *Tosca* costs £86; the same seat on the following afternoon for a double bill of *Ballet Imperial* and *Tales of Beatrix Potter* sets you back only £26. Both Companies contribute the same amount to administrative costs but The Royal Ballet often feels the poor relation, slotted in around the opera rather than vice versa. This sense of being out on a limb is compounded by the fact that The Royal Ballet's main base is miles away at Baron's Court in west London. Mostly it only comes up to Covent Garden for final rehearsals and performances rather than being a routine part of the fabric of the House.

Box Office receipts aside, the physical and artistic demands of ballet are very different to those of opera. Chunks of performance time suits the Ballet, rather than the opera system of a show followed by a couple of days rest. Because the Ballet has rotating casts of Principals – sometimes as many as seven different sets – the Company can dance the same production night after night after night. In December, for example, Fiona Chadwick and Michael (stage name Stuart) Cassidy danced the Sugar Plum Fairy and the Prince respectively in a matinée performance of Tchaikovsky's *The Nutcracker*, followed five hours later by Darcey Bussell and Zoltán Solymosi. With a couple of exceptions, even the most celebrated dancers are members of The Royal Ballet rather than famous names shipped in for individual performances. There is a strong team spirit, from the top to the bottom.

This sense of belonging is strengthened by the fact that many of the eighty-four-person company – even the stars – start in the Corps de Ballet and work their way up through the ranks. A few, such as Russian emigré Irek Mukhamedov who arrived from the Bolshoi Ballet in 1990, come in from outside. There are no hard-and-fast rules, but for most there is a well-worn path to follow – Artist (the Corps) to First Artist (Coryphées), Soloist to First Soloist, perhaps even up to Principal.

Now one of the ten male Principals in the Company, Michael Cassidy – who was diagnosed as diabetic two years ago – became interested in ballet when dragged along to his sister's classes. (Not an uncommon story, this, for the boys.) At eleven, he successfully auditioned for The Royal Ballet School based in Richmond Park, just outside London. He hated it at first, living away from his family. But time fostered a sense of belonging and within two years he was enjoying the supportive, albeit competitive, environment.

Only five of Cassidy's year were offered places at the Upper School in west London. For those not chosen, the sense of failure was made worse by the knowledge that they would lose all their friends in one go. Addresses were swapped, promises made to keep in touch, but the exclusivity of the world of ballet left little room for outsiders and people drifted apart.

Again at seventeen, a weeding out: of his year, Cassidy was the only boy to be offered a place in The Royal Ballet.

The word family is over-used in the theatre, but within the classical ballet world the dynamic is precisely that of a family. They have grown up with one another, the girls learning to police one another's calorie intake – competitive non-eating – and the boys building bigger and better muscles than the next man. As a rule, they live, work and socialize together. There are several romantic partnerships, a few husband-and-wife teams. Some reach the age of thirty never having known any other way of life.

Opera works in a very different way. This, too, affects the Company atmosphere. Leading singers cannot perform major operatic roles in long operas night after night without exhausting their voices. For them, the best schedule is a gentle run of performances, six or seven say, punctuated by three- or four-day gaps to allow the vocal chords to rest and recuperate.

Audiences expect to hear the world's greatest singers at Covent Garden – and they do. Glittering outsiders are flown in and rare indeed is the prima donna who works her way up to be plucked from the ranks. (The most celebrated exception is Kiri Te Kanawa, who was a junior principal singing small roles in the early 1970s.) There are sometimes alternative 'leads' programmed, but this is more to do with the very few dates top opera stars can offer to any one House: for some, their pencilled-in engagements already stretch well into the next century.

Not surprisingly, the atmosphere within the opera company itself is less intense, less intimate, than within the ballet company. It is more grown-up, somehow. The sixty or so sopranos, contraltos, tenors and basses who make up the Royal Opera Chorus are more like ordinary work colleagues. They see one another every day, rehearse and perform, but most have established independent lives as well. Unlike many jobs in the performing arts, a job in the Royal Opera Chorus brings security, a structured timetable, a regular place of work. Some have worked in smaller companies before auditioning, others have had wholly unrelated careers before eventually deciding to sing for their supper.

Voices mature slowly – and putting too much pressure on a developing voice can wreck it – so the youngest members of the opera company tend to be in their mid twenties, the older ones in their fifties. There is a system of encouraging in-house Principals, 'relatively inexperienced stage animals', as Royal Opera Director Nicholas Payne described two of this season's début performers, David Ellis and John Marsden. Both were gently being groomed and given one-liner solo roles – messengers, soldiers, known affectionately as 'spit-and-cough' roles – to help build their confidence and stage experience. Twenty years ago, Tom Allen was a House Principal.

Unlike most comparable theatres, every opera production at Covent Garden is rehearsed, even revivals that have been in the repertoire for years. After the singers have been preparing for three to four weeks in the Opera Rehearsal Room – occasionally without the big-name leads – each new show has a couple of weeks to try things out on stage. Everyone from the stagehands to the conductor needs to see the set made flesh, to practise cues and moves and embraces in situ. Once on Stage a round of rehearsals builds up to the opening night: just piano and chorus, but no lights, costumes or props; a *Sitzprobe*, where the Principals are lined up along the front of the Stage on functional chairs to strive for optimum balance between voice and orchestra; full cast and just piano; a technical rehearsal for lights, flies and special effects, all cued by the Stage Manager sitting at an electronic console in the Prompt (stage right) corner in the Wings. By the pre-General Rehearsal, everyone should be used to the acoustics of the red-and-gold horseshoe Auditorium; by the second, every last prop, every last move should be stage-perfect. Then, finally, comes the General Rehearsal, the equivalent of a Dress Rehearsal in spoken theatre.

Anxiety is often the dominant emotion. Shrill jokes and tense smiles are part of the mythology that if the General Rehearsal is a disaster then the First Night will be a triumph. The General is usually open to friends of the cast and crew and official supporters of the House – as well as press cameras – although everyone is issued with a health warning that it is a working rehearsal not a performance. Every new arrival on the Stage, every well-known aria or colourful banner, is met with a whir of shutter-clicking from the photographers peering round or through one another's tripods. Because much of The Royal Ballet's preparation has been done to the sound of a piano at its home at Baron's Court, when the dancers arrive in the House for their first Stage Rehearsal there is often an excitement about being in Covent Garden at all. Their first reactions are often as much pragmatic as aesthetic. Sure, that sweeping narrow staircase looks beautiful – but it will be impossible to negotiate in pointe shoes, just look at it.

Jane (stage name Madeleine) Mitchell and Beth Michael, attractive and energetic members of the Royal Opera Chorus, suggested that the heightened atmosphere backstage during a ballet rehearsal or performance was perhaps to do with testosterone levels. 'Beth and I are relatively young,' smiled Jane wryly, 'but if you look at the ladies chorus as a group they are not particularly a group of women that one would home in on as objects of sexual desire.' Beth pulled a speak-for-yourself face. 'They're not,' Jane emphasized, 'not as a group. But I am told by stage management, that sometimes the Armani suits come out for ballet and the stage crew shower and shave. We haven't witnessed this yet because we're never here, but apparently they really make something of themselves and stand in the wings a lot.'

Beth laughed. 'Usually we're wondering what the hell we're going to fall over next in the semi-darkness backstage. But usually it's a wire not a stagehand!'

'Management have got a job to do and I've got a job to do,
there's no need to get nasty about it.
They are open to ideas and we are in a good position
if we can come up with some good ones.'

Peter Coggon, Chief Union Steward for BECTU

O C T O B E R

In the centre of Richmond Park stands an elegant white building, a well-kept secret. At the end of a curving road, hidden from any but the most determined, it is the home of the Lower School of The Royal Ballet. Here talented children from eleven upwards, from all over the world – seventy-seven girls this year, fifty-one boys – come to test and nurture their dreams of a career in dance. Some, in truth more interested in football or film, are pushed by their parents. But most aspire to make it to the Upper School at Baron's Court. Then, who knows? If they are talented, if their face fits, if luck is on their side, perhaps they will make it into the Company itself and on to the Stage of Covent Garden. Viviana Durante, now one of the Company's star prima ballerinas, came to White Lodge from Rome at the age of eleven.

Built in 1727 as a Royal Hunting Lodge for George I, to step through the doors of the Lower School is to go back in time. The eyes of Richard Browne's familiar bronze of Dame Alicia Markova follow you around the entrance hall. One glass case holds a copy of *Piano Company Divertissements No 2*, another Margot Fonteyn's pointe shoes. And presiding over the calm is a bust of Madam herself, Dame Ninette de Valois, who founded the Company and School back in 1931 – known first as the Vic-Wells company, then the Sadler's Wells Ballet. It was she who, at the end of the Second World War, was invited to bring her dancers to the Royal Opera House as the resident classical ballet company. Both the Company and School were granted their royal charter in 1956, twelve years before the opera company.

In the vestibule downstairs a map of the British Isles is pinned to the wall, covered with sticky name tabs and arrows pointing to pupils' home towns and cities: those from abroad are listed separately. An old red phone box is tucked into a corner by the stairs for calls home. A notice is skewered to the noticeboard: PLEASE DO NOT CUT YOUR HAIR INTO A FRINGE – IT IS IN THE SCHOOL RULES THAT NO FRINGES ARE ALLOWED.

'Hold your tummy in, pli-é and turn, hold, hold,' dance mistress Christine Beckley projected over the sound of the piano. Through the windows, high up in the mirrored walls of the gymnasium, you can see the tops of trees. Twenty-one of the littlest girls, hair up in buns, were in pale blue leotards with tiny elastic belts, pink ballet shoes and white socks: the socks are much resented, the transition into a pair of 'proper dancing tights' an important rite of passage. In another class, slightly older boys stretched and jumped in short-sleeved royal-blue T-shirts, black pants and buckled belts. No glasses are allowed in class.

Wednesday, 13 October, White Lodge was expecting a visitor. Today, a new generation of young dancers faced their first major challenge as they auditioned for *the* Anthony Dowell, Director of The Royal Ballet. The production this Christmas was Tchaikovsky's *The Nutcracker*. Not only would some seventy children be chosen as party children, mice, soldiers, but they would need girls to dance Clara and boys to dance Fritz. Here was a chance not only to appear on the Stage of Covent Garden and gaze out into the famous Auditorium, but to shine in one's own right alongside some of the greatest dancers in the world.

An observational film crew had never before been allowed in to White Lodge. Michael Waldman and his BBC team were already in place and there was an air of excitement as Director of the School, Dame Merle Park, led in Anthony Dowell to the nervous studio. Backs were straightened, toes pointed out even further and a look of terror stamped itself on one or two faces.

Nine girls had been chosen to try for Clara. Each had very little time to persuade, as judgements were made about temperament and appearance as well as raw technical ability. Four names – Emma, Naomi, Maria and Helen – were called to dance the Act I *pas de deux* with a senior boy. The others were asked to rest by the barre. Emma looked older than the others. Too old perhaps? Naomi, clearly a favourite, had the right sort of spirit, pink cheeks

The Auditorium is crimson,
gold and ivory, the historic colours of the theatre. The gilded Victorian Proscenium Arch,
with its twisted columns, frames the Stage and the plush gold drop curtains – embroidered with
the Royal monogram – were first seen in 1911.
The domed roof is a startling cerulean blue, in the tradition of painting theatre ceilings
the colour of the sky in memory of their open-air predecessors.

and brown hair. Maria, half-Japanese, looked 'delicate and dainty', but was she perhaps too introverted to take control of the stage? Helen had a lovely smile and seemed confident.

Everyone in the room, from the pianist and teachers to the children themselves, was aware of Anthony Dowell's gaze. Phillip – who actually wants to be an airline pilot – is cheeky and talented. A possible Fritz? 'If he doesn't catch the ballet bug, then there's no point,' muttered Dowell. But perhaps a taste of the Stage itself might be a catalyst? That boy there, Grant, is it? He has a lively sense of theatre and would not look out of place in an Edwardian Christmas scene ....

It was dark by the time Christine Beckley pinned the sheet of paper to the notice-board. Red-and-blue tracksuits surged forward and, little by little, the names were passed back through the crowd: Alex and Grant had been chosen for Fritz, with Phillip as the cover (understudy); Naomi and Maria would dance Clara, with Helen as cover. As those who had not made it stared disappointedly at the list, then edged away, the hugs and amazed gulps of 'I don't believe it', started. Helen charged off to ring her parents, happy for the BBC cameras to come too.

How the six young dancers coped with the next couple of months would affect the rest of their lives. If they survived the pressure and relished rehearsing with professionals of The Royal Ballet itself, then maybe the opening of *The Nutcracker* on 17 December would mark the beginning of an historic career. If not, well ...

Back in Covent Garden, other people too were less than certain about their futures. The 1992 Warnock Report for the Arts Council had advised a radical overhaul of backstage working practices – a message endorsed by consultants Price Waterhouse, who had been commissioned by the Board, at the initiative of Sir Angus Stirling, to produce an independent assessment of the House's operating costs and practices – and this was to be the Season that words gave way to action. Job losses were rumoured and a general mood of worry was spreading.

There are three main unions in the Royal Opera House. Well over a hundred répétiteurs, music staff, ballet pianists and members of the orchestra are in the MU (Musician's Union) and there are nearly 150 producers, chorus members, dancers, producers and actors represented by Equity. But by far the most powerful union is the Broadcasting Entertainment Cinematograph Technicians Union (BECTU), representing some 300 people essential to the day-to-day running of the House. It was with BECTU that battle was to be done.

There was a genuine hope on both sides that negotiations could be civilized and fair. But the management message was uncompromising: if the House was to meet the challenges of

Endless miles of indistinguishable corridors
snake around the backstage area and back again. Peter Coggon, Chief Union Steward for BECTU –
who rolls his own cigarettes – contemplates the new NO SMOKING policy.

OVERLEAF The opening production of the Season
was Puccini's *Madama Butterfly*. Covent Garden saw the British première of the two-act Japanese opera
in July 1905, with Enrico Caruso as the faithless Lieutenant Pinkerton.

an uncertain future, then things were going to have to change. Flexibility was the key, not prohibitive regulation. The restrictive three-day week and consequent reliance on costly overtime would be tolerated no longer. (At one stage, it had been estimated that some ninety per cent of productions operated on overtime working.) Instead, a rostered shift system would be introduced. For both sides, management and unions, the three-day week was symbolically – as well as practically – the linchpin of the entire Stage Agreement. For management, it was a staff perk it could no longer afford. As Jeremy Isaacs put it: 'The whole notion of half a fortnight of leisure in which people are keeping fish-and-chip shops and playing golf is going out of the window.'

'The three-day week is extremely important,' explained electrics chargehand Chas

Spencer, one of the original architects of the three-day week system introduced in 1977. 'It gives us more time off and days together with our families. Because I go flying – we don't fly at weekends – I want the three-day week, or something like it.'

Under the new system there would be no more days given in lieu, no more overtime as a matter of course. Time, literally, was money. As things stood, if a rehearsal ran over by even sixty seconds then the resulting overtime payments, taking everyone into account, could run up to thousands of pounds.

Instead of a backstage area run by specialists, there would be multi-skilled project teams assigned to particular shows supported by a general running team on an as-and-when basis. What the management wanted was to breed a spirit of 'mucking in', people who would be prepared to do whatever was needed, rather than the current *modus operandi*: pockets of technicians who would only touch the lights, crew who would only move scenery but not sweep up, whatever.

In the Production Workshops, too, there would be change. Wigs required, on average, twelve hours of work, but maintenance during performances at the moment were treated as overtime: this would need to be looked at. The wardrobe system might change: current practice was that the production wardrobe was responsible for everything up to and including the First Night, but then the running wardrobe took over. Daft. In the new order, productions would be seen through from start to finish by one group of people, reducing the need for so many casual outsider dressers.

There would be a new dynamic grading structure to help people realize their potential and to reward achievement. And because some BECTU members, particularly the older ones, were bothered that they would be unable to master new skills – 'I'm a chippie,' worried one, 'not a lighting man' – everyone would be sent on training courses.

From now on there would be a crack-down on those attempting to abuse the system or who were off sick for long periods of time without adequate explanation. From his vantage point at the Timekeeper's Door – just along from the Stage Door proper in Floral Street – Ron Fennell oversees the comings and goings of the Stage crew. 'Everyone's a comedian here,' he joked, flicking his way through a thick wad of excuses and doctors' notes. 'More people are "ill" on Mondays.' By eight-thirty or so every morning, Ron has been given the timesheets, management's assessment of who's done what and when. 'You see this,' he said waving a piece of paper around, 'here you've got a man who's claiming for fifteen hours overtime – signed by the boss of a department – when he didn't even come to work at all!'

These were the changes, at any rate, that the Board wanted. And charged with making the Board's wishes come true was Richard Wright.

Very much of the old guard, Richard Wright had been John Tooley's Director of

Administration and admired him greatly: 'He grew up in the Opera House and was a dedicated workaholic'. Tooley had been General Director for nearly twenty years and deputy to the previous incumbent, Sir David Webster, for fifteen years before that. Not overly impressed with several of the recent House recruits to senior management, Wright was one of those who felt that Jeremy Isaacs had 'taken a few years, in my opinion, to understand what makes it tick'. (Or as one member of the orchestra rather unkindly put it, 'in the early days we lurched from unplanned triumph to planned disaster'.) Now at the end of his career, Wright was to leave at Easter having started off the process of consultation and discussion with BECTU. His job description would be broken down and interviews for his replacement – a full-blooded modern Director of Personnel – were scheduled for the beginning of December. Once his successor was in place, then negotiations would start in earnest.

The union side was led by Peter Coggon, the Chief Steward for BECTU. As an indication, perhaps, of how greatly management wanted things to go off without rancour, he had been given a year's sabbatical from his job as a Flyman – perched high above the stage – to see things through. Despite having been 'elected into the position through no fault of my own', he was in fact an effective negotiator. A good listener, prepared to be positive and not pre-judge, he understood that in reality BECTU's option was between a negotiated settlement and an enforced one.

'We don't have any industrial clout, really,' he admitted, rolling his own cigarette. 'The management have obviously got all the laws on their side. I mean, they've got the more powerful hand. If they wanted to impose something they'd be able to do it.' But he was optimistic about the spirit of the negotiations, that they would be good-natured. 'Though sometimes,' he added, 'things get a bit heated ...'

None of these backstage union anxieties could have been detected front of house though. On Friday 8 October the crimson and gold curtain would go up on the first new opera production of the Season, Wagner's *Die Meistersinger von Nürnberg*. A majestic opera, it is a rich and moral synthesis of young love and reflection on the nature of art and poetry. It had been a huge financial commitment – not least because of the sheer size of the cast and orchestra – and, to a degree, how it was judged would set the artistic tone for the whole Season. Music Director of The Royal Opera, Bernard Haitink, was to conduct this musical marathon for the first time.

'I like to belong to an opera house,' said Bernard Haitink, 'and apart from my Dutch accent I feel English.' He had arrived seven years ago, in 1986 – after twenty-five years with the Concertgebouw in Amsterdam – with relatively little experience in opera. One of his first tests had been to conduct the idiosyncratic Jon Vickers in Britten's devilish opera *Peter Grimes*. It was clear in those early days, reminisced one member of the orchestra, that 'he didn't feel confident handling all the large forces on the stage'.

A violinist by training, Haitink is someone who understands and respects the dynamics within an orchestra. One senior string player remembers that they were optimistic that musical values would be high under Bernard. Sure enough, shortly after he arrived, the acoustically-deadening carpet was taken up in the Orchestra Stalls. Haitink is now universally admired, loved even, despite a self-admitted predisposition to gloominess. As one journalist put it, 'he is finally enjoying an Indian summer after stormy beginnings'.

David Syrus, Head of Music for The Royal Opera, has worked at the House since 1977, under the Music Directorships of Haitink's predecessors Sir Georg Solti and Sir Colin Davis. 'Bernard's productions always are very smooth,' he explained. 'He is not into theatrical high drama and hysteria.'

With invitations to appear all over the world, Haitink is often away from the House though. His Associate Music Director, Sir Edward Downes – a nineteenth-century and Verdi specialist – takes up the baton in his place, supported by a succession of guest conductors. This means that the orchestra can get to work with a range of the world's top conductors in just one season: for many players, this is partial compensation for being stuck down in the Pit night after night, out of sight of the audience.

The triumvirate of Nicholas Payne, Jeremy Isaacs and Bernard Haitink himself resurrected a lapsed system of senior Music Department staff conducting an occasional show or revival. This Season, David Syrus was in the programme for a couple of performances of Mozart's *Die Zauberflöte* at the end of November. 'We're very grateful to the management,' he confirmed, 'for having the faith in us.'

As an indication of *Meistersinger*'s importance, perhaps, Haitink was to conduct all six performances. The explosive combination of his vision and Graham Vick's inspirational direction promised much, despite a running time of over five-and-a-half hours. 'Graham Vick leaves nothing to chance,' explained Terri-Jayne Gray, Opera Company Manager. 'Even if he checks the same point with you three times, he does it so there won't be a problem the next day.'

A House favourite, baritone Thomas Allen, as the irascible town clerk Beckmesser in Wagner's *Die Meistersinger von Nürnberg*. Directed by Graham Vick, it was the first new production of the Season. Each of the six performances in Autumn 1993 started at teatime, several hours earlier than usual, the audience picnicking in the two intervals. The curtain came down over five-and-a-half hours later.

A sparky Australian and organizational wizard, Terri-Jayne Gray arrived at the Royal Opera House ten years ago and worked her way up to the position of Opera Company Manager. She runs the schedule and it is down to her to make sure that the show gets on at night, that the singers are in the right place at the right time – and healthy. 'Some stars are very self-sufficient. It's enough for them to know that you're there if they need you. Others want you to do their shopping, their dry-cleaning, take them to the doctor. It's childcare, really.' Anyone who is ill is supposed to phone in by lunchtime on the day of the performance so that a replacement can be found. 'Some hang on and on because they don't want to give up the show,' she said with a good-natured raised eyebrow. 'Others stuff themselves to the gills with antibiotics, even though you shouldn't sing on antibiotics anyway.'

There were no last-minute changes to announce to the First Night cast of *Meistersinger*, no problems. The Stage Manager called beginners to the crowded wings. The orchestra, smart in their black and white in the Pit, had tuned-up and were waiting for Bernard Haitink to take the rostrum. Timpani players Nigel and Ronnie were trying to decide which cinema to visit during the performance ... with three-and-a-half hours between crash, bang, wallop cues, it was hardly worth hanging around.

By five o'clock the excited audience had finished browsing through their programmes. Handbags were comfortably perched on laps, coats had been rolled under seats in the Amphitheatre. The Auditorium was ready to hear Nancy Gustafson and Gøsta Winbergh sing the young lovers, Eva and Walther. A House favourite, baritone Thomas Allen, was playing the irascible town clerk Beckmesser and bass John Tomlinson the poet-cobbler Hans Sachs, perhaps one of the most inspiring, most human characters in any opera.

The House lights dimmed. Haitink's white baton fell, triggering bows across strings, the brass, the woodwind and percussion. Triumphant, majestic major chords as the Overture started, as it closed, a frenzy of triangle, glockenspiel and emphatic harmonies – tonic, dominant, tonic, dominant, tonic. As the performance strode on – six o'clock, eight o'clock, ten o'clock – thousands of faces in the audience marvelled at the power of it all – the candlelit hymns, the acrobats hanging from trapdoors high above the Stage, the costumed trumpeters on stage, the children, darting to and fro. 'Looks like a painting by Brueghel come to life,' a woman in the balcony decided, unpacking her sandwiches during the second interval. This was opera at its most thrilling, its most colourful, energetic and passionate. As the last chord thundered then faded, people threw themselves to their feet, percussive hands slapping out their praise. Flowers rained down on to the Stage.

On the Last Night – as the curtain came down on *Die Meistersinger von Nürnberg* for the sixth and final time that Season – the glow from the stage picked out many familiar profiles in the full Auditorium. Exuberant antics backstage resembled the on-stage rustic Dance of the Apprentices of Act III. Feathered hats were thrown high into the air, singers lifted one another's proud feet off the ground in delighted bear hugs as the luminaries gathered in the wings for their curtain calls.

'I hope you're not getting fed up,' joked Bernard Haitink to John Tomlinson as he prepared to take yet another bow. 'No, no chance,' he laughed. Jeremy Isaacs had come through from the Auditorium with Michael Portillo MP and his wife, to congratulate. 'You were wonderful,' Isaacs said as he embraced first Bernard, then Thomas Allen. The Portillos looked slightly embarrassed and hands were offered instead. 'I'd put Hans Sachs in charge of practically everything,' teased Jeremy. Then turning to Nicholas Payne, Director of The Royal Opera, slapped him on the back saying 'more, more like that'.

Five months later, *Die Meistersinger von Nürnberg* was nominated for the 1994 Olivier Awards and voted Outstanding Opera Production of the Year in the first *Evening Standard* Opera and Classical Music Awards. As Bernard Haitink himself reflected: 'It was a wonderful company achievement.'

Director Graham Vick's feet hardly touched the ground in October and November. A week after the triumphant First Night of *Meistersinger*, another of his shows had opened. His 1991 production of Mozart's *Mitridate, rè di Ponto* – written by a fourteen-year-old Wolfgang Amadeus – had won the 1992 Olivier Award for the Most Outstanding Achievement of the Year in Opera and was to be revived for six performances this Season with most of the original cast. Details from Japanese samurai, from Kathali dance and from native American kachina, were woven together in the extravagant costumes to create a stunning visual whole. 'A triumphant, virtuoso display,' raved the *Guardian*, 'a wonderfully imaginative solution to the problems of packaging opera for an audience today.'

There was a slight hitch on this First Night, though. Earlier in the day, news had come through that the first-cast kestrel was indisposed and would not be able to go on. Antibiotics not being an option, here was the chance for her cover – Jessie – to sparkle, sparkle, sparkle. But afflicted by either stage fright or malice, Jessie dangled from her perch during Act I and finally had to be removed from the stage after a great deal of flapping. Jeremy Isaacs later commented that he had been amazed at the number of bird-lovers in that audience on Friday, 15 October, all of whom had felt moved to write to him to complain ...

The Royal Ballet had taken the somewhat unusual decision to open its Season with a mixed programme of four highly individual modern works, two of them world premières by young choreographers in their twenties from the Corps de Ballet. Of course new

In traditional mould, Prokofiev's
Romeo and Juliet was the first full-length ballet of the Season.
Here, Rosalind Eyre, Ballet Mistress of The Royal Ballet, appears as Lady Capulet.
Many of the staff within the Company hierarchy mature into Character Roles: in time,
all princesses become queens, heroines become mothers.

OPPOSITE One of the world's best-known ballerinas,
Darcey Bussell, in her début as Juliet in October 1993.
Only a year after joining The Royal Ballet in 1988, she was already a Principal.

talent should be given a chance, intoned the cynics, but on the stage of the Royal Opera House on the First Night of its 1993/94 Season? Encouraging up-and-coming youngsters is all very well, but there are times and places …

Matthew Hart, twenty-one, joined the Company in 1991. He had already created one professional work for their sister company, The Birmingham Royal Ballet – as well as several shorter pieces – but *Fanfare* was his first commission for Covent Garden. Popular with peers and management alike, he is someone with talent whose face also fits. The General Rehearsal for the fifteen-minute *Fanfare* had gone well and everyone was cautiously optimistic. Boyishly roving around the front of the House, bounding up the red-carpeted stairs two by two, he seemed confident and excited: looking forward to seven o'clock. He even gave an interview to Michael Waldman and his television crew.

Things were not going so well, however, for William Tuckett. He had choreographed a couple of pieces that were now in the repertoire, as well as having created short works for The Birmingham Royal Ballet, the Rambert Dance Company and others. This was his third commission for Covent Garden. Three years older than Matthew, he was much more outspoken, critical of the ballet management and had a reputation as something of an *enfant terrible*. He was still in the Auditorium, listening to the Director of The Royal Ballet, Anthony Dowell, pensively voicing his worries. Brow furrowed, Dowell spoke softly and languidly. Tuckett's twenty-seven minute piece, *If This Is Still A Problem*, was not working, despite the best efforts of the dancers and the piano, cello and violin trio.

Sometimes moving into the House from the Rehearsal Studio in Baron's Court can bring unexpected difficulties. If the dancers rehearse and perform to recorded music, they are used to the exact speed, the precise pace of the phrases. But more usually they have been rehearsing to a tune played out on a piano. Obviously problems can then arise when they are faced with live musicians, the different timbres of woodwind, brass and strings. Used to the music following them – rather than its own internal cadences – the familiar notes suddenly sound distorted, wrong, to the dancers.

In the old days, the orchestra never had enough time to prepare either: Adrian Reed, now joint sub-leader of the Orchestra of the Royal Opera House, remembers rehearsing Prokofiev's *Romeo and Juliet* in the early 1970s only once before being driven into the Pit to face 'that fight scene full of semi-quavers'. But bit by bit, not least under the aegis of Barry Wordsworth, Music Director of The Royal Ballet (as well as for The Birmingham Royal Ballet), the quality had improved beyond measure. Accompanying the ballet was now no longer 'a really demoralizing event night after night', as Reed put it. And by the beginning of Wordsworth's third season in charge, the relationship between the musicians in the Pit and the dancers on the Stage had developed into a creative dialogue rather than a game of tag.

His success was acknowledged in March 1994, when he too was awarded an *Evening Standard* Opera and Classical Music Award for the outstanding Artistic Achievement in Dance.

But in today's General Rehearsal in the Opera House it was not the live music that was causing the problem with Tuckett's *If This Is Still A Problem*, even its title a hostage to fortune. In a programme billed as *White Hot and Different* the piece just did not fit – either with itself or with the three other works in the programme. Too late now. Perhaps the audience would at least enjoy the music Tuckett had chosen, the fluid cadences of Ravel, in contrast to the harsh serated sounds of Webern and Schoenberg for MacMillan's bleak ballet *Different Drummer*? But would the critics?

'Criticism likes to separate, to dislodge, to imply rivalries, to provoke jealousies,' Benjamin Britten once wrote to Michael Tippett. Most performers have one eye on the critics, even if they then dismiss their opinions as conservative, ill-judged or stupid. In ballet, there is a small competitive clutch of reviewers. Exceptionally well-informed, several of them are very elegant writers with the historical knowledge to put any dancer, any production, into artistic context. Others challenge orthodoxies, debate the essence of classical ballet and promote the need for a new tradition. A few not only review for newspapers and magazines but contribute to Royal Opera House publications as well: for example, the biography of Anthony Dowell printed in every ballet programme was written by the dance editor of *Time Out*, Allen Robertson, once also the *Daily Mail*'s dance correspondent. Some critics are so set in their views that it would be possible to pen their critiques before curtain up. 'They sit in extremely expensive seats – free – so I suppose they have to justify themselves,' said Keith Cooper, Director of Public Affairs and Marketing. 'Most of us would feel very uncomfortable having to sit and *criticize* a performance under those circumstances.'

None of this is wrong *per se* and the exclusivity of criticism in the ballet world is probably no worse than in drama, architecture, opera, whatever. But sometimes the sheer dead weight of expertise allows little room for spontaneity or fresh perspectives that might attract new audiences. What matters to most punters is not whether Australian Principal Leanne Benjamin's Titania is better than Antoinette Sibley's some thirty years ago, but if this year's production of *The Dream* will make their spirits soar. Only seven per cent of Covent Garden audiences are first-timers, and most of these are coming to the Ballet.

To a degree, the success or failure of a new production lies in the hands of this cliquish band of reviewers, whatever their tastes or temperaments. Just six days after *White Hot and Different*, the curtain would go up on Irek Mukhamedov and Viviana Durante in Prokoviev's *Romeo and Juliet*. A popular and well-known classical ballet, the seats would be filled even if the reviewers declared themselves bored. But experimental programmes are vulnerable, dependent on good reviews. *White Hot and Different* needed to sell more tickets ...

The First Night was cheerful, enthusiastic. The Royal Ballet was clearly happy to be back in the House for the first time in over two months. Even Matthew Hart's failure – on camera – to recognize Natalie Wheen, the doyenne of Radio 3 (she complimented him on *Fanfare* during the interval) failed to dampen his spirits. For some, though, the most exciting of the four pieces had been *Herman Schmerman*. A jagged explosion of virtuoso technique, it had been constructed by irreverent choreographer William Forsythe to a punchy staccato score by Thom Willems. It was less the sheer athleticism of the seven dancers that was the talking point in the foyer afterwards, though, than Sylvie Guillem. Brilliant, exact, dazzling, flame-haired, she had modelled a sleeveless black top designed by catwalk darling Gianne Versace. The top was transparent.

Anthony Dowell, though, had been right to worry about Tuckett's *If This Is Still A Problem*. The critics, the next morning, were unimpressed, dismissing it as a lot of wafting around without ever getting anywhere. 'Tuckett can do better than this,' wrote Clement Crisp in unusually restrained style, 'and The Royal Ballet should concern itself with guiding him.'

The ballet season opened on 23 October 1993 with a modern programme. Fashion guru Gianni Versace designed the costumes for *Herman Schmerman,* as modelled here by mercurial French ballerina, Sylvie Guillem.

'They are a very powerful bunch: the ladies help
with the Galas and selling tickets for Galas,
the men I look to for help in raising sponsorship.'

Felicity Clark, Director of the Royal Opera House Trust

NOVEMBER

Ticket sales and public subsidy alone have no hope of supporting a theatre of the size of Covent Garden. Wembley Arena can sell 80 000 tickets for a show, but the Royal Opera House has a mere 2000 chances or so per night to contribute towards its costs. However careful the husbandry, the sheer number of people involved in mounting live opera – and, to a lesser degree ballet – makes it an expensive business night after night after night. A quick flick through the booking programmes reveals that most productions or stagings have financial support from somewhere – Citibank or the Peter Moores Foundation, Dr Stanley Ho OBE, C St J or The Drogheda Circle.

There are two institutionalized fund-raising groups within the House, 'ladders of giving', as the Americans call them. Both – The Friends and the Royal Opera House Trust – are separate charitable trusts. Each appoints its own directors, and then evolves its distinct *modus operandi*.

The Friends of Covent Garden was founded in 1962 and now has some 20 000 members contributing many hundreds of thousands of pounds annually towards different productions and educational projects. At £40 a year (£16 for Junior Associates), privileges include priority booking, open rehearsals and *In Focus* study days and discussion evenings: November offered a whole Saturday on Mozart's *Die Zauberflöte*, in the Crush Bar; a Thursday evening on legendary choreographer George Balanchine and his *Ballet Imperial* in the De Valois Studio; and Ballet Master of The Royal Ballet Christopher Carr talking about how he helped translate the choreography of Frederick Ashton's *Tales of Beatrix Potter* from film into live theatre. The Chairman of The Friends is Bamber Gascoigne, member of both the Main Board and the Opera Board.

Beneath the half-page advertisement in some of the glossy red programmes for The Friends is one for the smaller Drogheda Circle. For a £1000 annual premium – or as a deed of covenant over four years – one can join an exclusive band of patrons sponsoring a particular production.

The next five pages of the programme are taken up with information about the Royal Opera House Trust: Premium Benefactors, Gold Star Members, Full Members, Country Members, it reads like a philanthropic A to Z of Britain's industrial might. *Pro bono publico.*

About sixteen per cent of House turnover comes from the Trust, The Friends and other donors and fifteen per cent of seats for every performance in the Orchestra Stalls and Grand Tier are reserved for selling to Premium Benefactor members. Critics claim that, while opera and ballet lovers cannot afford the price of a seat, these corporate patrons are only interested in buying a prestigious backdrop against which to do business and entertain clients. Elegant and poised, the Director of the Trust, Felicity Clark, admitted that the House does provide the 'opportunity to run into somebody to have, what I would call, a corridor meeting'. But she refuted the disparaging generalization that Trust members have little appreciation of the performers they applaud. 'I cannot answer for their guests, of course,' she added with some panache.

The Trust is chaired by Main Board member Jim Butler (ex-senior partner of the Royal Opera House auditors). His deputy, Vivien Duffield, is also a member of the Main Board and sits on the Ballet Board too. She is a formidable and determined woman. Trustees include Mrs Conrad Black, Mrs Gerald Ronson, Lord Sainsbury, Lord Young and Jeremy Soames. The name of the game is networking, the ability to open doors. Each Trustee has – or has access to – a great deal of money.

And herein lies the problem. There is an honest desire on the part of the people who work at the House to make themselves and their productions more accessible, more affordable by ordinary pockets. At the same time, fostering a sense of exclusivity seems to be essential if companies and wealthy individuals are to continue to support Covent Garden. One man at the Annual Trust Lunch was unapologetically candid: 'We like it *because* it *is* élitist –

OVERLEAF The Ladies of the Night. Mozart's
Die Zauuberflöte was an artistic – and financial – low-point for the House in November.
'Costumes à la Julian Clary,' sneered the *Sunday Times,* and several members of the Chorus
admitted they were embarrassed to be in it.

that's why people like to come here. One feels instinctively that the public subsidy should be used to increase accessibility, but not too much – because part of what makes this place special is that the audience is special. We're a company that wishes to be part of the British Establishment'.

Despite their names, trust and friendship are not always the most accurate words to describe relations between the two major fund-raising bodies. In 1992, the Warnock Report for the Arts Council suggested that the Trust and The Friends be amalgamated to better maximize opportunities and organization. The Price Waterhouse Report came up with the idea that perhaps all commercially-driven activities could come under the responsibility of a Director of Corporate Affairs: this might not result in greater cooperation, but at least there would be more efficient coordination overseen by an expert. Neither the Warnock nor Price Waterhouse suggestions were welcomed but, of the two, the Price Waterhouse compromise was the more palatable. Enter thirty-seven-year-old Keith Cooper. Head-hunted from English National Opera just half a mile down the road – and Opera North before that – he was the architect of several acclaimed marketing initiatives, not least the provocative campaign splashing stagehands and sopranos across posters to sell the ENO Company, not just the operas they performed.

Keith Cooper had arrived just before Christmas 1992 and had been astounded at the archaic attitudes. A spirit of Victorian philanthropy reigned supreme at the House, when what was needed was an aggressive, American-style approach to securing pounds and pence. 'What we are witnessing at this end of the market,' he sighed with a certain amount of exasperation, 'is a very distinct change in the way sponsorship is sought and found. We *are* a commercial organization and we've got to act like one. It is amazing that an organization that can be so incredibly adept at solving the crisis of the moment and getting shows on stage should be so completely inept sometimes at crucial aspects of income-generation.' He was also irritated by how possessive the two groups – the Trust and The Friends were of their contacts. Nobody wanted to yield any of their territory to the others. 'They understand the principle of bringing all fund-raising activities, all income-generating activities, under one management ... but they don't like it.' Cooper knew that it would be a long hard battle.

It was the Royal Opera House Trust which was organizing the Season's major fund-raising event, a glittering *Winter Gala* to be broadcast live on BBC television. Wednesday, 1 December, would see some of the world's top performers – from Plácido Domingo and Dame Kiri Te Kanawa to Darcey Bussell and Sylvie Guillem – perform in the presence of His Royal Highness The Prince of Wales and the Duchess of Kent. 'It is an absolute one-off,' said Mrs Vivien Duffield, Deputy Chairman of the Trust. 'I've been wanting to do it for fifteen years.'

As the November days ticked by, Vivien Duffield, Keith Cooper and Trust Director Felicity Clark had haggled for hours over the glossy programmes for the *Winter Gala*. Advertisements were juggled like a pack of cards, jostling for advantage in the sumptuous gold-edged pages: competitors must not be juxtaposed, loyal sponsors must be rewarded with premium positions. And what should be said about the Development and the Board's plans to overhaul the entire Royal Opera House? By the time usherettes were selling the programmes at the beginning of December, the development team would know whether or not Westminster City Council was going to grant planning permission for the next part of the House's building programme. In the end, Mrs Duffield decided that they could not risk printing anything too explicit, just in case there was a hitch.

The menu for the banquet had to be finalized too. So on Thursday, 18 November, Gail Ronson – another Trustee – had accompanied Vivien and Felicity to the kitchens of Mustard Catering. Smoothing crisp blue-and-white striped aprons over their immaculate clothes, plastic chairs were pulled across the kitchen to the long table. With white napkins serving as cushions, the three sat alongside one another to taste the beetroot crisps, the wild mushroom pasta, the Champagne – course after course after course.

In an attempt to spread applications for tickets more equitably throughout the House, prices had been kept down in the Stalls and inflated in the Grand Tier. (A prime box for the performance and the banquet would cost £6000, over twelve times as much as usual.) The ploy had failed, though, and demand was outstripping supply for the most exclusive seats. Who should be seated next to whom? Who should be given priority for the waiting list? Diplomatic decisions had to be taken.

The Finance Committee had some hard decisions to make, too. Stranded in Paris by snow, Jeremy Isaacs's unexpected absence from the meeting had given certain committee members the chance to criticize him for what they saw as a lack of follow-through control. Two major spring productions – one a ballet, one an opera – had gone over budget and the respective Directors had to explain to the Board why they needed more money. The situation was threatening to degenerate into an opera versus ballet bicker and, in a succession of meetings over the next few weeks, tempers flared. Sir James Spooner, Chairman of the Opera Board, mused about the likely effect of 'doing an Ernie Bevin and saying you can't bloody well have it'.

The Royal Ballet had been saving up for years, as it saw it, for a lavish new production of Tchaikovsky's *The Sleeping Beauty*. In part, this was one of the reasons it had opened its season with the modern programme *White Hot and Different* – fewer dancers, cheaper sets and costumes. A major investment, *The Sleeping Beauty* needed to be of a quality to last for twenty years or more. To that end, Maria Bjørnson – designer of Andrew Lloyd-Webber's

The Phantom of the Opera – had been commissioned to fashion a perfect fairy-tale ballet of fantastical colour and imagination, a *Beauty* to outshine all others. There was a huge cast to be costumed, not to mention several sets of Principals – eighteen costumes for Auroras alone. Special fabrics had been picked out, with subtle colours to be teased out by the Royal Opera House Dye Shop; diamanté, thousands of sequins, miles of delicate gold-and-silver threads would occupy the needles and thread of Wardrobe.

Several reputations were on the line. *The Sleeping Beauty* was Bjørnson's first ballet design; the world première would be in Washington in April, the first leg of The Royal Ballet's much-publicized American tour; Darcey Bussell would open as Aurora, in the footsteps of Margot Fonteyn; and, although staying faithful to Marius Petipa's original St Petersburg version, Director Anthony Dowell was restaging the founding father of choreography's classic.

Anthony Russell-Roberts, Administrative Director of The Royal Ballet, had justified the case for 'upping' the budget to the Board. Yes, admittedly Bjørnson's designs had been late. But *The Sleeping Beauty* was on budget for materials and it was only because the Production Workshops could not cope with the sheer volume of work thrown at them from all quarters that the Ballet Company needed to pay outsiders to help finish the work. Without more money, there would be empty containers crossing the Atlantic in March.

The main reason that the House workshops were under so much pressure was that another new production also needed the skills of the scenic painters, the milliners, the carpenters and the prop makers at exactly the same time. Friday, 4 March, would be the First Night of Janáček's *Katya Kabanova*, the House début-proper of ex-RSC director, Trevor Nunn. The Opera Company had also contracted *The Sleeping Beauty*'s designer, Maria Bjørnson, for this production.

Nunn and Bjørnson were old friends, but even though they had talked 'through every possibility of music and text as we saw it', he had nevertheless rejected her first designs. The schedule had slipped. If production values were not now to be threatened, it was essential that the Opera Company, too, should be allocated more cash.

The Main Board was astonished at the lack of coordination between the two companies. How could everyone have failed to notice – until the crisis was upon them – the huge and impossibly complicated demands being made on the House workshops? At the very next Ballet Board meeting the Chairman, Tessa Blackstone, was livid, directing her anger towards both Jeremy Isaacs and the Opera Company. 'I think this is a really appalling story of

Instead of the usual welcoming
crimson-and-gold curtains, the First Night audience for Janáček's *Katya Kabanova*
was confronted by a huge gauze half-concealing ghostly bridal figures.

incompetence,' she said sharply. 'What I particularly object to, as Chairman of the Ballet Board, is that Trevor Nunn can reject Bjørnson's designs and who suffers? The Ballet does.'

Nicholas Payne, Director of The Royal Opera, and not present at the meeting, was furious at the implied criticism. 'I thought bloody hell, why are they talking about this without me being there.' Supported by Jeremy Isaacs, he pointed out through gritted teeth – to the Opera Board – that the House could not expect a designer of Maria Bjørnson's stature to refuse commissions. If she had not taken on *Katya*, she might just as easily have accepted a job from some other theatre. And one could not force someone as eminent as Trevor Nunn to accept designs with which he was unhappy.

Bad-tempered recriminations rumbled on for weeks. Exactly how far should artistic excellence be compromised by lack of resources was one familiar refrain. Quality endures, was another, it is what marks out the Royal Opera House from the rest, and so on and so on. Thomas Allen's notorious scarlet thigh boots for *Don Giovanni* were mentioned. Again. La Scala had already expressed an interest in taking the production of *Katya*, Jeremy Isaacs revealed. If it looks tatty, if it does not work technically on their stage, then they will not want it and that is more money down the drain.

In the end, to the sound of rapped knuckles, both Nicholas Payne and Anthony Russell-Roberts were allowed to go over budget – less than either had hoped for, but extra none the less. It was too late to do anything else without jeopardizing the productions themselves. Main Board Deputy Chairman, Sir James Spooner, suggested that in future it would be impressed upon everyone commissioned by the House – however lofty – that budgets and schedules are carved in stone.

Money aside, the *Katya Kabanova* set had promised to cause problems from the start. The cold claustrophobic atmosphere of an 1880s Russian provincial merchant community had to be created, safely. The furrowed surfaces had to help the singers interpret their characters, not twist their ankles. 'The set's everything the crew hates, really,' worried Geoff Wheel, the Production Manager responsible for *Katya*. 'Metal, fibreglass, rubber. And parts of it are going to get wet.' There were two real horses – at a cost of over £8000 with handlers and assistants – which required special hoof-coverings so that they did not slip. (The cobs turned out to be too white for Maria Bjørnson's taste and had to be retouched in Make-Up.) Six-inch metal troughs were to be built under slats in the stage to collect the stage rainwater. And as the hunted Katya confessed her adultery in the last Act, a brooding crucifix, supported by scaffolding, had to collapse – without killing anybody.

The front of the set overhung the Orchestra Pit by eighty-five centimetres (thirty-four inches). Although unusual, it was not really a problem except insomuch that the design had failed to allow space for the Prompt Box. Seen as an old-fashioned device by many – and long-since abandoned by many opera houses – it is a small covered box that rises out of the Stage. Inside, as if in a play by Samuel Beckett, the eyes, nose, ears and mouth of a prompter are visible. Music Director Bernard Haitink, a traditionalist, likes a Prompt Box. Since *Katya Kabanova* is in Czech, he felt the singers would particularly value the reassurance of a prompter. Nicholas Payne, a modernizer, thinks it a stiffling, archaic system, a sort of 'hidden assistant conductor' that interferes with design. Warning shots in the battle of the old against the new.

'Prompting's very claustrophobic, a filthy job,' shuddered David Syrus, Head of Music. Now more often leaving it to more junior colleagues in his six-person department, he was prompting for *Katya*. 'You prompt preventatively, giving the line before it happens. Other-wise, if they dry it's too late.' It is not usually the language as such that causes problems, so much as idiosyncrasies of the production itself. Like a spoken play, directors often make cuts, sometimes even trim lines from performance to performance if something is not working. David Syrus and his team speak – rather than sing – the first few words of every cue. 'I spend most of every performance,' he smiled, 'watching the eyes of the person that's singing for signs of panic ... .'

In the end, a compromise was reached in *Katya Kabanova*: no unsightly Prompt Box in the middle of the Stage, but there would be a cramped cubby hole, complete with television monitor, hammered out of the bit of the set overhanging the Pit. The performers on the Stage could see only David's face, the orchestra his headless body.

On 14 November Nicholas Payne had the unenviable task of telling Trevor Nunn that his budget was being increased, but by only half as much as he had asked for. Notoriously difficult to contact, this time Trevor Nunn was in Los Angeles easing in his new production of Andrew Lloyd-Webber's *Sunset Boulevard*.

Having been through the revised budget with a tooth-comb and faxed a list of possible compromises, Payne was steeling himself. Although Nunn's Glyndebourne production of *Porgy and Bess* had come in to the House, *Katya Kabanova* was the first production that he had created from scratch for it. Everyone was keen for the relationship to work.

'Room 2676,' said Nicholas Payne's secretary, as Payne poured himself a cup of black

OVERLEAF **D**uring the final act of *Katya*, a brooding
orthodox cross and scaffolding collapse as the Stage rain pours down. Soprano Elena Prokina
is left standing alone in the blighted provincial Russian landscape.

coffee. Technical Director John Harrison, glasses perched on the end of his nose, was scribbling questions to be put. Jeremy Isaacs was propped thoughtfully against the door jamb.

In the event, Trevor Nunn showed a clear understanding that opera is, as he put it, 'an exercise in imagination as opposed to resource'. Productions, such as *Sunset Boulevard,* are immensely complicated to stage but because of the likelihood of long runs and large audiences it is at least feasible that the money spent will be recouped: a lot of dollars had been spent in Los Angeles, figures that made a mockery of his London budget.

It was money well spent on Janáček's *Katya Kabanova*, though. The design was inspirational. Even the crew liked it, despite its physical demands. Putting it in for the first time in February, members of the Nightgang were clearly impressed too. Introduced by Jeremy Isaacs near the beginning of his period of office as General Director, the Nightgang is a twenty-eight-person team who take over when the regular crew have gone home to bed. They work through the night, striking sets and getting things ready for the next shift the following morning. It was just past midnight. Some of the Nightgang were in blue Royal Opera House sweatshirts, others in plain T-shirts, most were wearing protective gloves and had toolbelts slung round their hips. Sure, it was very heavy and you had to watch out for fibreglass getting in your eyes, but designer Maria Bjørnson had done a good job. Clearly surprised to be asked on camera for their aesthetic opinion by Michael Waldman and his television crew, it was evident that they not only respected Maria but took pleasure in building so exceptional a set. 'She's very detailed and wants everything exact,' said one supporter as he scrutinized the drawings like an architect, 'but she is practical. It looks good.'

Trevor Nunn himself was due in at ten o'clock the next morning, Bjørnson half an hour later. Distinctive in jeans and jacket, Nunn strolled round his Russian village with Maria, testing angles and trying out uneven surfaces. Clearly delighted, he courteously thanked the crew for having got it in so efficiently. They had just been 'Trevored'. Nunn's sensitivity and attention to detail, coupled with a prodigious ability to charm, is legendary throughout the theatre world. Terrified of heights, chorister Elizabeth Sikora was dreading the moment when she would have to hobble across a narrow path suspended three metres (ten feet) or so above the set. In the frenetic atmosphere of this first Stage Rehearsal, Nunn nevertheless walked Sikora through her paces himself until she felt comfortable with the moves. She, too, had been 'Trevored'...

'I tend to think there are very few operas to which I can make a proper contribution,' Nunn told the BBC film crew several months later. He had wanted to do Ostrovsky's *The Storm* – the 1859 play on which Janáček's opera was based – during his eighteen years at the Royal Shakespeare Company, but the time had never been right. The chance to direct *Katya Kabanova* was too good an opportunity to miss, budget or no budget. And with a closing call

to arms to delight the subsidy lobby, he added: 'This is an expression of our culture, this is
what we believe to be excellent and it should be collectively supported because it is to do
with national identity and is of national significance.'

And when the critics finally got to see *Katya Kabanova* in March, they too were unanimous in their praise: 'A jewel of a performance ... Covent Garden at its peak,' glowed the
Sunday Times; 'Sensitively and powerfully conceived, finely tempered,' judged the *Observer*,
'admirably and movingly performed – opera at its best.'

But, still in November, things were about to get worse. It was time to batten down the
penny-pinching hatches. In an attempt to use his resources as effectively as possible, Nicholas
Payne had decided to buy in a Scottish Opera production of Mozart's *Die Zauberflöte* to fill a
last-minute hole. Several productions are mounted in association with international Houses –

this Season alone there were collaborations with La Scala, the Vienna State Opera and Teatro Comunale di Bologna to name but three – but it was less common to buy productions wholesale from elsewhere in Britain. It was cheaper, obviously, than originating one's own. At the same time, it would help ensure that there was a wide range of new shows for the Royal Opera House to run alongside the big investments and familiar revivals. In theory, this could be a responsible way of meeting both artistic and financial goals, exactly what the Warnock Report had ordered. The House had 'junked' its own rather dated production of *Die Zauberflöte* so this combination of opera and circumstance seemed the ideal opportunity to put this theory to the test.

Nicholas Payne had hired Andrew Parrott to conduct and borrowed the sets, costumes, design and director lock, stock and barrel. It opened in the middle of November for fourteen performances. The experiment was not a success, despite the indisputable talents of Amanda Roocroft as Pamina. '*The Magic Flute* is a black hole into which two centuries of intrepid interpreters have vanished,' jibed Peter Conrad in the *Observer*. A vaudevillian, almost slapstick, production – which had been sung in English and designed for the more intimate Glasgow Theatre Royal – it simply did not work on the spacious stage of Covent Garden. The Ladies of the Night looked like something out of a bad Dashiell Hammett movie – 'costumes à la Julian Clary' sneered the *Sunday Times* – and several members of The Royal Opera Chorus told the BBC documentary film crew that they were embarrassed to have even been in it.

With only three performances to go, *Die Zauberflöte* was unlikely to make its target budget. The House had not even sold as many programmes as expected. On average, the programme sellers would expect to shift about 1000 copies a night for an opera performance, perhaps 700 or so for a full-length ballet. For the 1993/94 Season, it was experimenting in pricing up programmes for new productions, £5 as opposed to £3 for a revival. It had been successful for *Meistersinger*, but the *Flute* audience seemed unwilling to part with an extra £2.

Box Office failure aside, what also was at stake was Nicholas Payne's first attempts to broaden the variety of music on offer. Trying to move beyond what he called 'big band Mozart', he had an informed interest in the sort of authentic sounds – 'emaciated noise' as one orchestra member put it – championed by both Andrew Parrott and Paul Daniel, who had conducted the first Mozart opera of the Season, the revival of Graham Vick's *Mitridate*. Payne had already made it clear that he was even considering inviting specialist ensembles to the House in the future for Mozart and Purcell.

Most of the string players would cite Mozart as one of the hardest composers to play well. So for the orchestra, the prospect of suddenly being asked to play their largely non-authentic instruments in an authentic manner – different bowing, little or no vibrato – was absurd, particularly in a theatre the size of Covent Garden. It was not a technique to be mastered overnight. At the end of November, the orchestra committee voiced its reservations. It was an even-tempered meeting, but Nicholas Payne made it clear that he would continue to pursue a more radical agenda. A few months later he was explicit about the scale of the battle between himself and the traditionalists when his plans to woo John Eliot Gardiner and his Orchestra of the Age of Enlightenment for a production of *Così Fan Tutte* for 1995 fell through. 'It is a major defeat for me,' Payne admitted, 'because I've pushed it through in the teeth of warnings and opposition from every corner, and I did so because I thought a number of people needed to be taught lessons about sticking in ruts.'

In many ways, the most triumphant night of the month was actually not at Covent Garden at all. As the *White Hot and Different* dancers took the stage for their performance on 16 November, Dick Ensor, the Chief Executive of the Development, was squaring up for his performance – albeit a non-speaking one – in the chamber of Westminster City Council. A collection of specialist property developers, money men and senior figures within the House, the Development Board had been set up to oversee operations and to ensure that Phase II of the redevelopment went through. Westminster City Council was by now a home-from-home for Dick Ensor and his team. They had been there many times before. Tonight they were hoping to be granted planning permission for the southern corner of James Street.

Leading down from Long Acre to the market itself along the back of the Opera House, James Street is a semi-pedestrianized road with an old-fashioned hot chestnut brazier smoking there every winter. At the moment, the corner was home to several market traders, traditional stall-holders selling towelling robes, army surplus, leather bags, whatever. The Royal Opera House wanted to replace these pitches with a purpose-built home for The Royal Ballet, with colonnades mirroring those opposite in the piazza. The sooner building started, the sooner the Company would be able to move up to Covent Garden from its base in West London. The James Street corner was crucial to the beginning of the Phase II programme.

Westminster City Council was a familiar stomping ground, too, for Jim Monahan, a long-term opponent of the Royal Opera House Development scheme. An architect himself, Monahan had links to the House through his father, an eminent ballet critic, who had once been married to the Director of The Royal Ballet School, Dame Merle Park. As Chair of the Covent Garden Community Association, Jim challenged the right of the Opera House to deprive market people of their livelihoods, as he saw it, and believed the whole

development to be inappropriate, inefficient and ugly. 'It looks like sin,' he had said to Jeremy Isaacs of architect Jeremy Dixon's designs, 'like an old shoe.'

Until now, the Council had refused to allow anything more to go ahead unless the House could prove that it could finance the entire Phase II scheme from start to finish. It did not want the development to proceed in fits and starts, perhaps remaining half-finished if the money dried up. But now the Council had decided to waive the relevant Section 106. The development of the James Street corner would be considered in isolation.

Despite attempts from the Labour group members in the chamber to get a further deferral – on the grounds that they were being asked to make decisions that should be part of the Government's national arts policy – the Council voted the scheme through. It was a landmark for the Development. Asked afterwards for his opinion by Michael Waldman and the documentary film crew, Jim Monahan said he was not in the least bit surprised that the goal posts had been moved. 'The Opera House has powerful friends,' he said.

On the opposite side of Floral Street
to the House itself is the Dye Shop. Diva the dog and polaroid canine friends watch as trousers,
shoes and tutus are transformed from yellow to ochre, blue to aquamarine.

Home-from-home. Having started her career
with The Royal Opera in the early 1970s, on 1 December 1993, Kiri Te Kanawa
topped the bill with Domingo, Guillem, Bussell and Mukhamedov at the Tchaikovsky *Winter Gala*. Two
million people watched the live BBC2 transmission.

OPPOSITE On his first flying visit of the Season,
Plácido Domingo not only took possession of the Stage at the *Winter Gala* but took up the baton in the Pit
as well. A prime box for the performance and banquet afterwards cost £6000.

'All the big names are friendly. Plácido Domingo gives fans a performance at the Stage Door before he comes in, says hallo, signs books and poses for photographs. I'm not singling him out – lots of them are like that.'

Peter Meade, Head Stage Door Keeper

DECEMBER

The shops in Covent Garden piazza had dressed their Christmas window displays several weeks ago. Now it was the turn of the Royal Opera House. Wednesday, 1 December, the night of the Tchaikovsky *Winter Gala*.

At eight a.m., Peter Meade, Head Stage Door Keeper, opened the grille and took in the milk. One hundred pints. 'If they don't get their milk, it's drama time,' he joked. Unobtrusive glass doors on the Floral Street side of the building, it is the busiest Stage Door in Europe. 'It's questions, questions, questions,' mock-sighed Peter as he prepared to sort through the three sacks of mail, all needing pigeon-holing by initial or department. 'It's the nerve-centre of the building, so anyone who wants anything comes here. We occasionally take in pets, and one night we had three dogs as well as a baby crying in a cot ... '

Peter Meade – and his team – not only need encyclopaedic memories for names and faces, but also immediate recall as to who is welcome backstage, who is not – no enemies, tax collectors or rival agents. 'Bigger names require shielding and tact,' commented Peter. Fans try to leave programmes and books for autographs. And some, knowing little about their idols, are more interested in the physical attributes of the performers than their handwriting. 'The lady fans come mostly to see the gentlemen of the opera,' he smiled, 'and it's gentlemen who come mostly to see the gentlemen of the ballet ... ' The House even has its own phantom of the opera, a woman who claims to control the Ballet telepathically.

Today the atmosphere at the Stage Door will be even more frenetic than usual. Not just one or two of the world's leading performers, but an entire celebrity cast will be gathered under the roof of the Royal Opera House for the *Winter Gala*. Royalty too. 'You do have to put on a performance,' Peter grins, clearly relishing the day's work ahead. 'As somebody once said, it's the longest running show in the West End.'

Terri-Jayne Gray, Opera Company Manager, is in her office, her bleeper silent for the moment. 'We're pretty careful about security here,' she muses, 'in a laid-back sort of way.' It is usually only on performance days that the big names attract crowds of fans. 'The person we have most trouble with is Pavarotti. Women just throw themselves at him, shoving roses in his face.' Terri-Jayne, who is barely 1.5 metres (5ft) tall in heels, has to help rush him through the throng and in through the stage door in one piece ...

For her, too, the *Winter Gala* will be very labour-intensive. A very long day and night looking after not one but several world-class singers, even if Pavarotti is not one of them. They all have to be got happily into the theatre, hand-holding during the performance if necessary, shepherding her flock to the banquet afterwards. 'It's trying to slice yourself up amongst them all,' she grimaced.

In the Auditorium below, cleaners vacuum and polish as Deputy Chairman of the Trust, Vivien Duffield, sweeps into the Crush Bar to inspect the floral displays. Everything is to have a wintry character, St Petersburg come to London. Paul Dyson, who has done flowers for the House for about eight years, admits – when pushed – that Mrs Duffield is 'demanding, but creative'. Fresh silver birch, white roses, lilies, fir cones, the foyer looks beautiful. She is pleased, although the smell of pine is a little overpowering. 'They'll sneeze,' is her first comment. Interviewed by Michael Waldman and his team, she is cautiously optimistic, excited. (Rightly so – the *Winter Gala* raised £700 000, nearly £100 000 more than anyone expected.)

With more than a touch of self-reference, the documentary film crew starts to film its BBC colleagues setting up for the live television broadcast.

It is dark now. In the road outside everyone is waiting for the Prince of Wales to arrive. The cold air smells wealthy, perfume superimposed on the more usual fragrances of Bow Street. Limousines silently discharge jewelled women and groomed men, long skirts and dinner jackets *de rigueur* for once. A crowd of passers-by lingers to watch, kept at a safe distance by the police. For tonight only, just like the old days, the splendour on the Stage will be mirrored by the opulence of the audience.

At seven-thirty, the face of James Naughtie fills the screens of BBC2 and the strains of

Abdul Jaulim, one of the two Greencoats –
Flunkeys – relaxing in the canteen. Their red-and-gold Georgian uniforms
were donated many years ago, second-hand, by Buckingham Palace.

the National Anthem curl up into every corner of the Royal Opera House. Over two million watch at home.

The Auditorium has been transformed by drapes and lights from its usual dominant crimson to white. Classical Russian scenes, the spirit of snow and winter and a portrait of Tchaikovsky dominate the stage as the glittering talents of members of The Royal Ballet and The Royal Opera fill the theatre. Velvet, sequins, tulle. Plácido Domingo takes possession of the Pit as well as the Stage. The voice of Dame Kiri Te Kanawa floats out, sublime. The only modern note is Sylvie Guillem, dancing *Herman Schmerman* in her transparent Versace top.

Abdul Jaulim and Jonathan Kustow, the two Greencoats, are waiting backstage. Known as Flunkeys, and dressed in their distinctive Georgian wigs and red uniforms (donated many years ago, second-hand, by Buckingham Palace), they present the Principals with their flowers at the end of every show. They hold back the curtain, too, for the individual calls and gather up the flowers thrown on to the Stage by the audience. In the Wings tonight there is row upon row of bouquets for the women, bottles of Champagne for the men. The audience, on its feet and applauding, does not want the show to end. Jonathan and Abdul go back and forth, back and forth.

In the Banqueting Hall afterwards the Chairman of the Royal Opera House, Sir Angus Stirling, launches his speech of thanks on to a sea of famous faces: not only tonight's stars, but actors, politicians and writers, women and men whose names are known even if their features are not. White cloths cover tables for ten, each with a gold swan as a centrepiece. The red of the AIDS ribbon pinned to William Tuckett's dinner jacket matches the flowers.

Wednesday night gives way to Thursday morning. Terri-Jayne Gray is now sitting on the stairs: 'Like Cinderella, waiting for them to finish so I can get in a cab and go home ... '

Thursday, 2 December, eight a.m. Peter Meade, Head Stage Door Keeper, opens the grille and takes in the milk. One-hundred pints.

It is not business as usual for everybody. John Seekings, Assistant Technical Director, has to make the first face-to-face management presentation in the union negotiations. He is dreading it. BECTU has been given draft documents for discussion, but destructive rumours are growing and there is a certain amount of misinformation being traded. Call it politics, call it internal public relations, it is important to get this official pitch right.

The BECTU audience clearly does not consider this the season of peace and goodwill. John Seekings is clearly nervous as he stands before his workforce, clutching his papers. His Technical Manager Dave Reid sits frozen on his left. As the speech is delivered, shuffling and fidgeting from the floor soon give way to undisguised irritation, hostility even. Is multi-skilling up for negotiation, is the three-day week? It sounds more like a *fait accompli* rather than a negotiation.

There is no applause and, as the workforce files out, the mood is sceptical. 'There's nothing to say,' says one electrician who has apparently already been told that he will be working under a new contract next season. 'I'm more confused now,' says another, 'than when I went in.' 'Everyone's floundering about,' Chief Steward, Peter Coggon, says drily.

Elsewhere, rather than seeking a straight replacement for the Director of Administration Richard Wright, management is intending to do away with this title and instead appoint a Director of Personnel. It needs someone to inaugurate new, athletic industrial relations in the House, someone who can steer the negotiations through with BECTU, and fashion a flexible modern workforce to carry the House through the difficult two-year closure period. It has to be someone with experience of large institutions, someone who believes in effective relations with the trade union without being bullied by it. Most of all it has to be someone with courage, someone who can embrace change and move the House forward.

Over twenty people have applied for the job of Director of Personnel, including Richard Wright's deputy Judith Vickers, who is currently Personnel Manager. This has resulted in a long list, then a short list of four, then a shorter list of two. The selection party, a heavy-weight team, gathered in Jeremy Isaacs's office: Board member Bob Gavron, the new Direc-tor of Finance Clive Timms and Isaacs himself.

One of the applicants is Mike Morris, the Personnel Director at ITN, and the architect of its radical restructuring programme. He knows BECTU and, in his own words, relations had remained cordial despite having done 'unspeakable things to them'. He has also worked with Clive Timms (who had left ITN only months earlier) and come across Jeremy Isaacs in a professional capacity much earlier in their respective television careers. Morris is an out-sider, someone with a fresh perspective who would not treat House traditions as sacrosanct.

If Morris is appointed, the Royal Opera House would be able to keep Judith's expertise and insider knowledge as well. The politics will be slightly awkward, of course, but she would ease his passage through the drawers of suffocating paperwork for the negotiations thus far. They decide on Mr Morris.

Over the phone, they metaphorically shake hands and agree an April starting date.

Thursday, 16 December, Jeremy Isaacs is sitting in his office waiting for the phone to ring. He does not look relaxed. Despite a financial surplus over the last two seasons, the Royal Opera House has been warned by the Arts Council to expect a reduction in its annual grant. The 1994/95 budget is already straining at the seams – the first two operas of the new Season *Der Ring des Nibelungen* and Richard Eyre's new *La traviata* will be expensive – and there is an unexpected question mark hanging over a substantial donation the House has been banking on. A Hong Kong businessman had promised over two million pounds to the Opera House. It has received half of it, but there is now the possibility that he might be

OPPOSITE 'There is the opportunity to run into somebody to have what I would call a corridor meeting.' Felicity Clark, Director of the Trust, which masterminded and carried off the *Winter Gala*.

OVERLEAF The 'dreaded furry beasties' of *Tales of Beatrix Potter,* live on stage for only the second time. Mr Jeremy Fisher with friends Peter Rabbit, Piggling Bland, Squirrel Nutkin, Mrs Tiggy-winkle, Johnny Town-mouse and Jemima Puddle-duck.

THE ROYAL BALLET SCHOOL

Sandy Kennedy, one of the three-person team
at the Stage Door in Floral Street. Over 1000 people pass through every day, wanting anything
from stamps or matinée tickets to pet-sitting services or a shoulder to cry on.

unable to honour the second tranche. If the Arts Council carries out its threat of a two per
cent cut, then current plans will become financially impossible.

Relations between House and Council nose-dived after the publication of the Warnock
Report in June 1992. A stiff civility had barely been maintained, but under the careful guid-
ance of Sir Angus Stirling a Joint Action Committee was convened to try to get the two
institutions talking again. After all, the Opera House is the Council's biggest client – and you
cannot just refuse to speak to your bank manager. The idea was that every six weeks or so,
usually at the Arts Council headquarters in Great Peter Street, there would be coffee and
dialogue about a specific issue: finance, repertoire, redevelopment and so on.

It was like musical chairs. The Arts Council personnel were being shuffled and reshuffled
into jobs and out again – hardly the structured environment within which productive working relations could be rebuilt – and meetings achieved little, at worst the House playing the
recalcitrant adolescent to the pompous parent routine of the Council.

The phone finally rings in Jeremy's office. Mary Allen, Deputy Secretary General of the Arts Council, relays the news that House has cash standstill for next year. Pushed, she admits that in fact no one has received a cut in subsidy, despite the Council's warnings. 'Is this another U-turn?' asks Jeremy towards the end of the conversation. He is not a fan of the double-act of Chairman Lord Palumbo and Secretary General Anthony Everitt. 'They say yes to everything, in effect saying yes to nothing.' Then, with barely suppressed irritation, he adds: 'They constantly deny us the funds to enable us to carry out their express wishes'.

The Box Office is having money jitters of its own. The Royal Ballet has been performing a Double Bill – Balanchine's *Ballet Imperial* and 'the dreaded furry beasties' of Beatrix Potter, as Jeremy Isaacs calls them – since 20 November. Perhaps because schools do not break up for nearly a month or so, bookings have been slower than expected. By the middle of December they have picked up a little, but the situation is aggravated by the fact that the Box Office telephone system seems unable to cope with the nature of the Christmas audience. Many people who are ringing are not regular visitors to the House, so almost every conversation has to include an A to Z of prices and sightlines: 'If you're a senior citizen, student, unwaged, Musicians' Union, Equity, Incorporated Society of Musicians and Stage Pass Member, Westminster ResCard Holder you can buy one ticket from the foyer Box Office one-and-a-half hours before the curtain goes up'. 'No? Under eighteen? Could I just explain that there are some seats in the Auditorium with restricted view ... ' Every call was taking over twice as long as usual. Some would-be punters tried for days and failed to get through, finally giving up under the illusion that by now the show must be sold out. There are, needless to say, complaints.

To help avert the knock-on effect that the *Potter* congestion is having on bookings for other productions, Keith Cooper, Director of Public Affairs and Marketing, took the decision to hand the show over to a professional ticket agency. A few of his staff denounced this move. How can it be right that members of the public would have to pay more for their

OVERLEAF Christine Beckley (in mirror)
taking a morning class at White Lodge with some of the youngest pupils. Maria (extreme left)
was one of the girls chosen to dance Clara in *The Nutcracker*. Her face looked out from the posters
all over London advertising the Christmas show at Covent Garden. No glasses are allowed in class –
and it is school rules that hair must not be cut into a fringe.

tickets — commission on top of the price of the seat — because of their antiquated House Box Office systems? More complaints, even though Keith had already agreed that the House will pick up the tab.

Scribblers — some, not all — gave the impression that *Tales of Beatrix Potter* has been the staple Christmas diet at the Royal Opera House for generations. In truth, it only appeared on stage for the first time in 1992. Frederick Ashton had first choreographed Mrs Tittle-mouse, Mrs Tiggywinkle and friends for the 1972 film, but had resisted all attempts to stage it live at Covent Garden. Now, five years after his death, the animals were back on stage. They are all-but exterminated by some, not least a bilious *Financial Times* reviewer denouncing the whole exercise as nothing more than money-grubbing: 'I cannot believe that adults should be expected to spend seventy minutes watching pork chops on the hoof and assorted vermin scampering about the Opera House Stage, masked, padded, in the throes of rampant cuteness'.

The audiences, however, love the cute critters. Children, young and old, are enraptured by the flashing colours of the huge masks, Jeremy Fisher's yellow striped trousers and Squirrel Nutkin's whiskers. They eat their ice-creams and enjoy themselves, and think about Christma and fancy dress parties.

Over the past two months, the six children from The Royal Ballet School, chosen as soloists for *The Nutcracker*, have been rehearsing their parts with members of the company. While their classmates were learning to be party children or mice or soldiers, Maria, Naomi and Helen have been at Baron's Court, as if real members of The Royal Ballet. Grant, Alex and Phillip have been mastering the part of Fritz.

Keith Cooper and his Marketing Manager, Ian Temple, decided to use a photograph of Maria for the poster advertising *The Nutcracker*. Her thoughtful face is now looking out from posters all over London. Even though an A cast, a B cast and covers (understudies) were also picked back in October, any two of the children might now be picked to dance with Lesley Collier and Irek Mukhamedov on the opening night.

Tchaikovsky's ballet is the perfect magical children's fairytale world come to life: toy soldiers, large nutcracker wooden doll, the spirit of Christmas. A huge cast and many special effects — snowflakes, trap doors, flying sleigh, spectacular Christmas Tree which grows before the audience's eyes — it is the sort of busy split-second timing show that the stage crew enjoy.

Helen is chosen to dance Clara at the first Stage Rehearsal. For many of the children, it is their very first time backstage at Covent Garden. Shepherded by Christine Beckley, with her distinctive ballet dancer's waddle, they crocodile their way up the cramped red staircases from the dressing rooms into the Wings. Excited and chattering, they look like any other gang of schoolchildren. 'No talking once we get on stage,' they are reminded. Most of them,

anyway, are awed into silence by its sheer size. Tipping their necks back, some glance up into the Flies. Others peer into the Auditorium, imagining what it will be like when the House lights have gone down and their parents, brothers and sisters are sitting there in the audience, waiting. They breathe it all in, as if they might never again have the chance. The less timid ones lightly finger the corners of the set. Blocking is well under way so that everyone will know where they are supposed to stand at all times. 'Can I have the naughty children please?' barks Miss Beckley.

Sitting in the Auditorium with fellow ballet mistress Shirley Grahame a few days later, Christine Beckley is listening to Anthony Dowell and Sir Peter Wright, Director of The Birmingham Royal Ballet. Each girl and boy has had the chance to take possession of the Stage, but now a decision has to be made about who will dance Clara on the First Night, who will be Fritz. All four adults are conscious of the huge responsibility they are laying on these twelve-year-old shoulders. In the end, though, they are unanimous. Each child will have their turn, but Naomi and Alex will open. Maria takes the disappointment bravely, saying she is looking forward to her chance at the first matinée.

By five o'clock on Friday, 17 December, most of the cast is in the House. Some are still in the canteen, but most are warming up or double-checking that their props are in the right place in the Wings. The ballet dressing rooms are small, cramped even, compared to those of the opera. Common to both is the formality, the politeness. Backstage, all women are Miss, regardless of age or inclination. Dressing Room 1 lists Misses Collier, Conley, Rosato and Brown on the door; Miss Benjamin, Miss Bussell, Miss Tranah and Miss Valtat share No 2. Mr Mukhamedov is allocated No 8 with Mr Carreño, Mr Cope and Mr Solymosi. Squeezed in elbow-to-elbow, fourteen are sharing the Girls Corps dressing room. It looks like a school PE changing area. The rooms are like living scrapbooks. Good-luck cards are stuck to mirrors, bowed wooden shelves are piled high with pointe shoes. Costumes hang on rails, their owners' names scribbled on cards skewered by safety pins. Unless especially complicated, dancers do their own make-up and hair. So blusher, huge bushy make-up brushes, eyeliners, fag-ends of lipsticks and scatterings of hair grips clutter every available surface. There are odd boxes of matches and packets of cigarettes here and there, and a half-drunk can of Diet Coke. A tannoy speaker, high up on the wall, booms out the calls. 'Ladies and Gentlemen, this is your fifteen-minute call, your fifteen-minute call. Thank you.'

In the children's dressing rooms, the teachers are giving out First Night presents. Then, with her hands protectively on her young charge's shoulders, Christine propels Naomi into the Wings. Philip Mosley, who is dancing the nephew in the *pas de deux* with her, comes over to say good luck. There is an atmosphere of crossed fingers, friends whispering to 'break a leg'. They, too, want to do well, to *not* be the one who falls over or drops their Christmas present prop.

The Nutcracker performance goes so fast. Already here is the Transformation Scene, as battalions of little mice are spirited up from under the Stage in a swirl of mist. The trap-door is only just shut in time. 'By the skin of our teeth,' hisses Miss Beckley in the wings, banishing unwanted visions of her pupils plummeting back through the hole. Everyone in the Wings is watching. Naomi's mother, father, brothers and even old dancing teacher are out front in the audience. Naomi looks wonderful, natural and graceful, and as if she is enjoying her duet with Philip. 'It couldn't be better,' whispers Christine, 'I'm all tingly.' Face flushed, Naomi is exhilarated as she runs off stage at the end of Act I. Trotting down stair after stair, adrenalin loosening her tongue, she is back at the dressing room in next to no time. As she walks through the door, her friends start to clap and cheer, wrapping her generously in their little girls' arms.

With Christmas over, it will be hard to go back to being just another pupil in school.

'The cigarette girls should be a good strong tan ...

This is southern Spain, tell them that, they're not on holiday.'

Ron Freeman, Wig and Make-Up Master

JANUARY

WH Auden once wrote: 'No good opera plot can be sensible, for people do not sing when they are feeling sensible'. For some, the contrived plots and archetypal stories of opera are irrelevant to life as they know it. But since an uncertain première at the Opéra-Comique in 1875, Bizet's *Carmen* has become one of those operas whose vibrancy, passion and sexual tragedy redefines barriers by transcending them: the *habanera* rhythm, jealousy, tobacco leaves, sex. It was the first production staged by Karl Rankl's newly-formed Covent Garden Opera Company in January 1947.

Now, in January 1994, the new Carmen, American mezzo Denyce Graves, has just arrived in London. Graves grew up in troubled south-west Washington with her brother and sister. Her mother was so determined that the children would stay out of trouble that she arranged a water-tight schedule of after-school activities, including Thursday night at the local Baptist church. 'I was never exposed to anything classical or refined, not at all,' confided Graves in her gravelly relaxed voice. 'But I loved to sing and I came from a family that loved to sing – mostly gospel music.' At first her view of opera singers was the traditional stereo-type: 'That Wagnerian soprano with the long braids and the breast plates, the brass boobs and all that. But I began to read some of the opera stories – I'm completely a soap-opera addict, I'll confess – and I became fascinated and intrigued by them. They spoke to me and made sense to me.'

By 1994, only three years out of music college, Denyce Graves had already sung with

Maestro Muti at La Scala and with Plácido Domingo in Los Angeles, and her sultry Carmen has a growing reputation within the opera world. But this was her Royal Opera House début and, to a degree, she was a Box Office gamble.

'A Carmen must have a vibrant voice and the natural personality,' Nicholas Payne insists. 'There's nothing more embarrassing than a Carmen who acts sexy – you've got to be it.' No worries on this front. Tall and glamorous, Graves exerts as powerful a magnetism on those offstage as on the soldiers with whom she flirts in Act I. 'Absolutely gorgeous,' admitted one member of the orchestra, 'nice voice too.'

Keeping up a relaxed commentary as she takes possession of her dressing room, Denyce lays out a breakfast picnic – orange soda, potatoes, a boiled egg and a fruit salad. Today's ten-thirty Stage Rehearsal is a blind date with the first of her three Don Josés, Neil Shicoff. For the last four performances, his place will be taken by Plácido Domingo. 'Now I have to do something to this outfit to sort of sharpen it up a little,' she mutters as she shoves down the white material of her gypsy blouse to create an impressive cleavage. 'At first, I thought I looked like a milkmaid, you know. But the bodice is beautiful.' It is her favourite costume, not least because the other three are so heavy, so restricting. Then, clutching a half-eaten toasted ham sandwich in one hand and a box of false eyelashes in the other, she sets off down the unfamiliar corridors in search of Ron Freeman in Make-Up. Occasional interrupted chords echoed from the tannoy as Michael Waldman and his film crew tail her up and down half-flights of stairs.

Denyce Graves and Ron Freeman establish an immediate rapport. Denyce continues to nibble as Ron applies her foundation. (There are still few black divas, so many carry their own base make-up.) They chew over the relative merits of grease and powder before relaxing into their respective Jessye Norman anecdotes.

'So I said: "Miss Norman, what can I possibly say to you that you haven't already heard a million times?" And she said: "My darling, I'm sure you can think of something."'

'That's very good, that's very good,' mutters Ron as he reaches for the ringing phone to answer a question from one of his team about how dark the women of the chorus should be. Back to his Carmen. False eyelashes top and bottom or top only?

'Looky uppy!' instructs Ron, eye-liner in hand.

'I love it when he says that!' she chortles. 'It's a real social education being down here with you, Ron.'

Flyman Francis Shiels up
in the Flies high above the stage, lowering and raising scenery and backcloths.

Occasional trills, bizarre glissandi, escape from Denyce's throat as she applies her own lipstick. They agree that it is a very personal thing, lipstick.

The rehearsal goes well, by and large. As one of the cigarette girls eats an orange up on the balcony, the Chorus Master begs the female choristers to think 'sweetness rather than volume'. Richard Sadler, one of the three assistant stage managers for Opera, has managed to juggle a fistful of smoking cigarettes in to the wings — props for the flamenco dancers amongst others — without setting fire to the building. 'I've hardly ever come across a woman opera singer smoker,' jokes Opera Company Manager Terri-Jayne Gray, 'but lots of basses smoke — they say it drops the voice ... ' The horses behave, too, and are rewarded with Polo mints by their toreador handlers. And a nosebag hung on the corner of a cart has proved the perfect hiding place for a dustpan and brush, just in case nerves get the better of the equine performers on the night.

The only slight hitch is the running time, eleven minutes late by the first interval. Terri-Jayne has to decide whether to officially extend the session — damage-limitation costing a packet in overtime — or else take a chance on getting the curtain down in time. 'Will they leave the Pit?' she asks Cliff Corbett, the Orchestra Manager. The last thing they need is the entire orchestra packing up and leaving bang on two-fifteen, finished or not.

Carmen is a busy show for the stage crew, but it is not slow scene changes that are being blamed for the potential over-run so much as the pace of the music. Denyce herself had found the pace a little slow. Perhaps it could go a little, you know, faster on Monday? The only *Carmen* that lasts all night, was the in-joke sneaking its way round the House. 'Have you heard the one about Carmen,' spluttered a technician, 'who died of old age.'

Carmen's opening performance, Monday, 17 January, is scheduled for the last night of the outreach initiative Hamlyn Week. (The First Night proper would follow on the Friday.) Sponsored by the City of Westminster and the Paul Hamlyn Foundation, Hamlyn Week is — as the booking programme cautions — '*only* for first-time attenders of opera and ballet at the Royal Opera House' and tickets are much reduced in price. Since 1986 it has attracted over 84 000 people and this Season ticket stalls were set up in all sorts of unusual places (such as the Elephant and Castle Shopping Centre in South London) to help attract as wide an audience as possible.

As the audience of first-timers assembled, Denyce Graves unpacked her warm-up kit: a

'I have to do something to this outfit
— sort of sharpen it up a little.' American mezzo Denyce Graves as Carmen —
the first of the Season's three wild gypsies — flirting with the soldiers.

humidifier, an Oletta Adams album and a bag of apples. 'When I put a sign on the door saying PLEASE DO NOT DISTURB, everyone assumes that doesn't mean them,' she remarked, in good spirits. After a few gentle scales, arpeggios, she felt confident. 'I slept well. I feel good, had a nice long walk.'

On stage, everything started well – cymbals, then the short overture preluding the array of famous tunes to come. In Act I, the receptive audience was amazed by this seductive Carmen, the way she flirted with the soldiers, the way her gypsy costume swished dramatically as she moved. But in the wings, during Act II, it pretty soon became clear that something was not quite right. Denyce's voice was starting to slip away. She had felt so good earlier. Why was her throat suddenly feeling so sore? Determined as she was to finish the show, by the end of the next Act she could barely sing out. Jeremy Isaacs was roused from his seat and, pushing his way through the red plush curtains, he made an announcement from the front of the stage. Miss Graves was unwell, but would carry on. There was an immediate burst of clapping from the supportive concerned audience.

Act IV features the ten-minute duet introduced in the opera's opening bars, then comes the final confrontation between Carmen and Don José. Unable to accept that Carmen no longer loves him, Don José draws his knife. Down comes the blade and Carmen sinks dying to the floor. Neil Shicoff and Denyce Graves had worked on this scene many times. But, this time when the curtain closed, Denyce remained motionless on the stage. Everyone in the wings tensed. Had she fainted? Should anyone do anything? After what seemed an eternity, but was actually no more than a minute or so, Denyce hauled herself to her feet. There was tumultuous applause from a sympathetic audience, but it was a very disconsolate Denyce who accepted a bouquet from the Flunkey. All that she cared about now was being well enough to sing on Friday.

The next morning, Terri-Jayne Gray managed to get hold of their top ear, nose and throat specialist in Harley Street who could see Denyce at three o'clock. Terri-Jayne suspected that Denyce had not fallen victim to some mysterious virus, but had 'over-sung a bit, worn herself out by the end of the opera. They all get terribly excitable in rehearsal and overdo it,' she added.

Later that afternoon, the ENT man diagnosed a touch of vocal chord oedema, but no actual laryngitis. His advice to Denyce was to go home and not to talk. It was rest, not drugs, that would do the trick.

Back at the House, Terri-Jayne was thoughtful: 'Voices will go earlier and careers will be shorter because people drive themselves on all the time to do bigger and better roles. For example, voices dry out terribly in aeroplanes, yet singers are on and off them all the time'.

On Thursday, 20 January, it was clear that Denyce would not be able to sing Carmen the next night. 'It's many years since we've lost a performance through illness,' Terri-Jayne assured everyone calmly, as she set to work to find another Carmen. If Denyce had been unable to finish Monday's performance, then the rehearsal understudy would have been called upon. But for leading roles the House always brings in another named singer for performances: after all, when people have paid so much money, they do not expect to see Jo Bloggs from the chorus in the leading role. Terri-Jayne and her colleagues had twenty-four hours to find someone and get her to Covent Garden.

'It needs quite a heavy mezzo voice and it's a really difficult role. You can't have a dumpling singing it,' she explained as they dialled singer after singer. There was no one available in England. 'You're limited in Europe,' she continued, 'because they don't always sing the role in the language in which it was written. In German houses, for example, they often sing everything in German.' In Toulouse, a husband wrongly thought that his wife might be interested in the role. In the end, a relatively unknown Marseillaise mezzo accepted. 'All we know is that her name sounds like a tin of fruit,' said an obviously relieved Terri-Jayne. 'She must be fairly confident, though, because she said she didn't want to work with any of the other artists ... '

On Friday, 21 January, eight-thirty in the morning, a terse notice – DENYCE GRAVES IS ILL – was stuck in the window of the Box Office. When it opened at ten o'clock, staff read the name scribbled on a scrap of paper to customers. MAGALI DAMONTE. No one was quite sure how it should be pronounced.

In a matter of hours, a very formal and neat Frenchwoman would make her début on the Stage of Covent Garden in a production she had never seen with a cast she had never met. Denyce Graves's costumes seemed to fit well enough, although Magali Damonte pulled up the white material of the gypsy blouse modestly. Next, she was shown four colour photos of the set by one of the House Staff Directors, Stuart Maunder, and was talked through the score and blocking with the répétiteur. Damonte's English was limited, as was the staff's conversational French. The hours passed in compromise and inexactitude.

Already in black tie, conductor Jeffrey Tate arrived at five o'clock. Introductions over, they started rehearsing at the piano in Damonte's dressing room, now vacated by Denyce Graves's apples and soul music. It was five-forty. The curtain was due up at seven.

Every singer, from the Principals to those with 'spit-and-gob' solo roles of no more than

OVERLEAF The Arrival of the Toreadors
in Bizet's *Carmen*. Horses were used for some performances, their handlers costumed and on stage too.
The horsebox was parked in Floral Street and as a reward for not fluffing their lines,
the horses were rewarded with Polo mints.

a line or two, are given two seats in the Orchestra stalls for the First Night. At the Stage Door, Denyce Graves was gracious as she handed back her free tickets. She had not heard of her replacement.

Magali Damonte was nervous and came in early for one of the *habanera* verses. Some said there was no sense of sexuality, no sense of the heat and passion that the storyline requires. Few critics made allowances for her last-minute mercy mission, several dismissing her voice as 'too small'. At least her accent was perfect.

Injury is the *bête noire* of the Ballet Company. Voices are vulnerable instruments but can, to a degree, be cared for and kept safe. The dancers' bodies, however, are put through such extraordinary physical punishment day after day after day that it is almost inevitable that they will crack and slide under the pressure. And in ballet, as in sport, there are some people who are more easily damaged than others. As Aileen Kelly, one of The Royal Ballet's physiotherapists, explained: 'They're always working in that interface between physical pain and exhaustion.' It is only when it is physically impossible to continue that they take notice.

At a rehearsal in February 1993, eleven months ago, Michael Nunn felt a small pain in his heel. Aileen told him to rest for a couple of weeks, but this did not help. Perhaps it was an Achilles tear? After three months in plaster Nunn felt well enough to go to Istanbul with the Company during the summer. The pain persisted. Acupuncture, cortisone injections, anti-inflammatory tablets, massage – nothing worked. There was only one option left.

Nunn is twenty-six, another Royal Ballet School graduate who has worked his way up through the ranks. A dancer liked by choreographer Kenneth MacMillan, he could have expected to make First Soloist during the 1993/94 Season. Instead, he was sitting in his house in Chiswick waiting to go to the Portman Square Hospital to be operated on by Mr Strachan. Racks of CDs and an electric guitar were propped in the corner of the sitting room. A pair of crutches leant idly against the wall, waiting.

Over the years, Mr Strachan, had done repair work on many, many dancers. 'When I saw Dame Margot Fonteyn's feet for the first time,' he confided, 'I couldn't believe she could stand up.' Unlike Nunn, who was pessimistic, Strachan was confident that the operation would be a success. But he issued a caveat: it was not the physical scars that would cause Michael problems, but the mental ones inflicted by six months of rehabilitation. So often, injury divorces a performer from their entire life. Michael will not only miss the *Dance Bites* tour planned for the next month, but also the prestigious American tour in April. Left alone in London, his girlfriend and most of his friends would be away for over five weeks. Michael was determined to recover fast enough to be back with the Company for its two-week stint in New York in July 1994. In the event, he was still not fully fit by the beginning of the next London Season in November.

Other people's injuries had given chances, though, to a young First Soloist, Adam Cooper, another of The Royal Ballet School alumni. Several times Adam had found himself on stage at a moment's notice taking the place of injured Principals.

Friday, 28 January, was the First Night of the revival of MacMillan's full-length ballet, *Mayerling*. The temperamental and brilliant Hungarian Principal, Zoltán Solymosi, was injured. Irek Mukhamedov did not feel able to step in at such short notice, Nunn was injured, Jonathan Cope was not yet step-perfect and none of the other five Principals knew the role. That left Adam Cooper, who had stepped in for Zoltán in *Mayerling* once before. His partner on that occasion, Viviana Durante – alongside Bussell and Guillem, one of The Royal Ballet's crowd-pulling ballerinas – would now partner him again tonight, replacing Leanne Benjamin as Mary Vetsera.

Actually 'Super Cooper' was starting to feel rather exploited as he bailed out the Company time after time without being made a Principal in his own right. At the end of the tiring Christmas run, he had screwed his courage to the sticking point and asked for a meeting with Anthony Dowell. What he had wanted was a clearer idea of how he could expect his career to develop over the coming months. But instead of congratulations he had received a carpeting for having mucked around in a performance of *Ballet Imperial* a few days earlier. Any affectation – 'mincing' in the words of one Corps dancer, 'limp-wristing, camping it up' in those of another – is frowned on by the Ballet management.

Now at five-thirty, about to go on yet again in place of Zoltán after a mere ninety minutes of rehearsal, Adam Cooper was still in the canteen with friend and fellow dancer – and choreographer – William Tuckett, whose *If This is Still a Problem* had been one of the four pieces opening The Royal Ballet Season back in October. The curtain was due to go up on *Mayerling* in two hours.

A functional and airless environment – despite the relentless turning of the huge ceiling fans – it is only snatches of music over the tannoy that proclaim this a theatre canteen. Plastic salt-and-pepper pots and Sarson's vinegar, decorate the tables. The drab walls are not improved by the wicker flower baskets and, apart from the blue Fosters ashtrays in the Smoking Section, the only splashes of colour are the vending machines and the gold-rimmed emerald mirrored menu board with the words ROH Staff Restaurant printed across the top: soup 40p, beef curry £2.25, custard or cream 25p. On the counters are tall glass jars stuffed with different raw pastas destined never to be cooked – swirls, strings, green and cream shells – and one jar containing black-eyed beans.

Many of the people working behind the counter are black, those sitting at tables almost all white – Britain reflected in miniature. It is crowded, but no one mixes that much. An occasional head-setted and miked stage manager bears away a paper plate covered with cellophane; one or two members of the crew sit at one table, a couple of members of the orchestra at another; a few ballerinas, in civvies, nip in to buy a piece of fruit or a yoghurt; a male dancer takes in carbohydrate in the form of a calorie-defying lasagne before going off to squeeze into his costume.

Adam Cooper and Willliam Tuckett are in the Smoking Section with the documentary film crew. Unlike Irek Mukhamedov, Adam did not really feel in a position to refuse to go on. 'It's a matter of absolutely vile politics,' growls William who is dancing Count Larisch tonight. Neither was aware that the opera company had been through exactly the same experience just a week earlier.

In the Amphitheatre Bar, Bert was disappointed that Zoltán was not dancing, but sure nevertheless that he would enjoy his evening all the same. Despite being partially deaf, Bert has been coming to the Royal Opera House every night for the past twenty years since his wife died. He used to be a maintenance engineer at Hackney Town Hall, and before that worked for Glaxo, but says that because he does not drink, drive or smoke he can afford to buy a restricted-view seat right up at the top in the Upper Slips for between £2 and £7 a night. He brings his own binoculars. Insisting he is not musical, he explains that he prefers 'something bright and colourful' to Wagner or Strauss. For him, the foreign languages are part of the excitement of a night at the opera. And the dancers are terrific. 'Mind you, I'm not surprised they have accidents with the capers they cut.'

It was nearly seven-thirty now and Adam Cooper was standing in the wings, elbow-to-elbow with other members of the cast. Music Director Barry Wordsworth had come backstage to wish him luck before taking up his position in the Pit. Everyone had their fingers crossed for him.

Adam was nervous and took a while to get into his stride. But, bit by bit, stamina, adrenalin and commitment took over. With its brooding emotional score by Liszt (as orchestrated and arranged by John Lanchbery of *Beatrix Potter* fame) a sense of diseased sexuality pervades

Kenneth MacMillan's *Mayerling*,
a ballet of adultery, drug addiction, murder and suicide.
Zoltán Solymosi, pictured here with Leanne Benjamin, was billed
to open on 28 January. Injury forced him to pull out
hours before curtain up.

Mayerling. Addicted to drugs, to violence, to flesh itself, the Prince is a fated man, at first seduced by – then possessed by – his daemons. It is a role that, above all others, demands acting skills in partnership with power and technique, the Hamlet of ballet roles. It was during the First Night of the revival of his staging in October 1992, that choreographer Kenneth MacMillan collapsed and died from a heart attack.

The ballet staggered remorselessly towards its climax, a wild dance. The Prince and his seventeen-year-old lover, Mary Vetsera, writhed with increasing desperation. And as Cooper dragged Viviana Durante up-stage to the draped bed, the Auditorium seemed to be holding its breath. Adam put the gun to her head, pulled the trigger, then shot himself, centre stage.

The Principals took their individual calls, their black silhouettes exquisitely symmetrical in the spotlight in front of the red curtains as they bowed or curtsied to the audience. A few flowers were thrown, the Flunkeys brought on the bouquets. Finally, the applause died away and the house lights came up in the Auditorium. People stretched arms and legs, others looked for cloakroom tickets or pushed their empty chocolate boxes under their seats.

Anthony Dowell made his way backstage to deliver his customary post-mortem to the cast. Very measured, low-key almost, he thanked the forty-odd dancers – nobles, officers, chambermaids, ladies-in-waiting – and congratulated Viviana, Fiona Chadwick and Adam. Then, quietly, he added another couple of words that Adam was almost too tired to take in as he turned to go back down to his dressing room.

Would everyone please give a warm Covent Garden welcome to Mr Adam Cooper, newest – and youngest – Principal of The Royal Ballet.

'My costume for *Chérubin* is one of the most comfortable
I have ever had and it's rubber. It was made by the maker
of the costumes for the Batman film, lined with
lycra and fitted to me. Brilliant!'

Beth Michael, Soprano, Royal Opera Chorus

F E B R U A R Y

Thursday, 17 February, the Arts Council of England headquarters in Great Peter Street. The Joint Action Committee (JAC) was meeting to discuss the Development plans. Jeremy Isaacs, in one of his seemingly inexhaustible supply of silk ties – this one black-and-white stripes – had lined up with Keith Cooper, Director of Public Affairs and Marketing, Finance Director Clive Timms, and a few members of the Development Board.

Facing them across the claw-footed table was the Arts Council contingent of the JAC, Chaired by Peter Gummer and supported by Deputy Secretary General, Mary Allen. On the wall behind them was an enormous orange board – *Highlights of the Year 1992/3* – testament to the beneficence of the Council. It dominated the room. Acronym after acronym, ENB, ENO, Arts 2000. In one corner there was an illustration of a macho crouching man with a machine gun ...

The atmosphere was irritable. Everyone was trying to give an impression of candour while actually playing their cards close to their chest. Back in December Lord Palumbo, outgoing Chairman of the Arts Council, had spoken out in favour of a brand new opera house on the South Bank and criticized Covent Garden's priorities: 'There is no air-conditioning and often not a lot of leg room. These, and the backstage facilities, are what the Royal Opera House should be concentrating on, not a major redevelopment'.

Peter Gummer was twitchy at the lack of financial information being given. 'There's no point in being nervous,' retorted Jeremy Isaacs pugnaciously, 'and asking us for something we cannot give you.' The House had already made it clear that it was intending to apply to the newly-established Millennium Commission for public funding for a third of the cost of the redevelopment (a sum not less than £45 million, perhaps as much as £60 million). The public appeal would be led by Vivien Duffield and Lord Sainsbury – personally shouldering a sizeable chunk of the financial burden – and the remainder would be raised through realization of the House's property assets.

The 1993 Lottery Act had given hope to Britain's hungry arts establishments. Proceeds from a weekly National Lottery would be used to finance five good causes: the arts, sport, national heritage, charitable projects and initiatives to mark the year 2000. At this point, though, the whole thing was an exercise in speculation. The Millennium Commission had made it clear that it did not want to see business-as-usual-ideas dressed up with the thin veneer of celebration, but beyond that information was thin on the ground. No one involved seemed sure to which fund major arts institutions should apply, Arts or Millennium. Lottery tickets were due to go on sale in November 1994, but no lottery operator had yet been chosen. Perhaps no one would play, or at least not enough people. But these were mere details and no obstacles to the imagination. So the Tate Gallery, the South Bank, the Cardiff Bay Opera House Trust all dreamed ...

The Royal Opera House felt that its case was as good as anyone's for a slice of the Millennium Fund. Applications were probably not going to be invited until the beginning of 1995 – only two years before the House would shut down – but it had been waging a gentle PR campaign so that the Commission was already well aware of Covent Garden's realistic, not to say inspirational, plans for transforming its old Victorian theatre.

Although the Arts Council were Trustees of the scheme, it would actually be up to the Millennium Commissioners to assess the financial viability of projects. Jeremy Isaacs and his team, therefore, did not think that February's Joint Action Committee had any right to ask for specific figures for the cost of the redevelopment. 'It's not your money,' growled Isaacs. 'All we're asking you to do is to agree with the bare bones of the thing, that it is a sensible thing to try to achieve and that we're behaving in a financially responsible way in trying to bring it about.' Coffee cups were raised to lips, spoons clinked in the civilized white saucers, sentences floated up into the air. They traded countless words, but neither side wanted to trade specifics.

Increasingly exasperated by the House's assumptions, Peter Gummer finally pointed out that it was wrong to assume that the Council had allocated resources to Covent Garden during its period of closure: 'It's not inconceivable that you should close down,' he said. Keith Cooper looked inscrutable, Sir Kit McMahon, Chairman of the Development Board, looked exasperated and Jeremy Isaacs looked as if he were about to lose his temper. 'Ridiculous. Patrons do not give money for the bricks and mortar,' thundered Deputy Chairman, Sir James Spooner, 'but to support their world-class opera and ballet companies. If there are no performances for two years, three years, whatever, then sponsorship will simply dry up.' 'It's the responsibility of the Arts Council to attend to its clients and to tender to their needs,' reinforced Isaacs rumbustiously. 'It would be *lunatic* to allow the artistic resources of the House to be dispersed.'

Politics aside, one reason why the House was reluctant to put figures for the redevelopment plans on the table was that the plans needed revising. Again. A few months earlier, Stanhope Properties – previously unconnected with the Phase II scheme – had been invited by Sir Angus Stirling and Jeremy Isaacs to give an independent assessment of the design. They had recommended several major amendments, not least the ditching of the House's idea to turn property developer. The original intention had been to build an office block and make money from commercial lettings, but the market had collapsed and London was now saturated with expensive unlet properties. Stanhope had suggested using the space in Russell and Bow Streets for the House's administration offices and workshops.

These were major revisions to the plans, not just tweaking, so everything would have to go back to Westminster for approval. Never mind the Joint Action Committee, it was touch-and-go as to whether the designs and figures would be ready for the Council meeting in April.

It was artistic touch-and-go in Covent Garden, too. Nicholas Payne, Director of The Royal Opera, had 'had to take it on the chin for a difficult few months' at the January Opera Board meeting. 'Productions we bought in, which had looked fine when we saw them elsewhere,' he sighed, 'didn't fulfil our expectations when they arrived. We went into the deals with our eyes open, but you can't altogether predict how these things will travel.' Despite having reallocated funds from *Meistersinger* – which had come in impressively under budget – to help towards the overspend on *Katya Kabanova*, the Opera Company figures were not looking terribly good.

Chérubin was due to open on Valentine's Day. Massenet's *comédie-chantée* – about what happens to the young Cherubino after the curtain has fallen on him at the end of Mozart's *Le Nozze di Figaro* – had been premièred in Monte Carlo on 14 February 1905, but rarely performed since. Not only would this be its first-ever professional staging in Britain, but it was also Nicholas Payne's first personally chosen – rather than inherited – production. The

accomplished American mezzo Susan Graham was to sing the eponymous hero – what is known as a 'trouser' role – and the up-and-coming young Romanian soprano Angela Gheorghiu was to play Nina. Payne had put the direction and design in the relatively young hands of Tim Albery and Antony McDonald, a House début for both. To round things off, the highly-respected and experienced Gennadi Rozhdestvensky was to conduct. 'He has a sort of Russian technique that means he can do anything with his hands,' said orchestra sub-leader, Adrian Reed. 'A real genius conductor.'

In most operatic productions there is a tension between the musical and dramatic elements. To a degree, the rehearsal process itself is the settling of disputes. The key to a really outstanding production is the quality of the resolution reached, ideally the spark between the Pit and the Stage leading to an inspired artistic cohesion rather than a drab compromise. For Nicholas Payne, *Chérubin* was, 'if you like, an antidote to the German stodge of *Elektra* or the *biftek fiorentina* of Verdi'. For Tim Albery, too. But it had long been evident that there was a fundamental incompatibility between their vision of the opera and Rozhdestvensky's.

Tension increased. On Saturday, 5 February, during a Stage Rehearsal with orchestra, things came to a head. Although extremely popular with musicians, Rozhdestvensky – Noddy, as he is nicknamed – is notorious for missing Piano Rehearsals. Because of this, he had ploughed on during a certain passage leaving the singers behind, not knowing that it had been decided that there would be a repeat. An irritated Tim Albery had snapped that if Rozhdestvensky had bothered to turn up to rehearsals he would have known about the repeat. An apology was demanded. None was given. Rozhdestvensky walked out, leaving the Royal Opera House to orchestrate a damage-limitation exercise.

When arranging a last-minute cover for an opera role, the first port of call for Terri-Jayne Gray, Opera Company Manager, is Peter Katona, Artistic Administrator of The Royal Opera. An essential part of his role is having worldwide knowledge of which productions are being staged and when at his fingertips, a mental card-index of performers' voices, languages and repertoires. Katona was able to bring to mind one of the very few people who knew the score of *Chérubin*. Just over an hour after their transatlantic telephone conversation, the Canadian conductor Mario Bernardi was on the only plane leaving Toronto that night. He

Conductor Mario Bernardi leans against the Pit Rail during the General Rehearsal of Massenet's *Chérubin*. He is conferring with Bram Gay and Cliff Corbett, Orchestra Director and Manager respectively. An hour after being phoned, Bernardi was on the last flight out of Toronto that night after the previous conductor had stormed out just days before the First Night citing 'irreconcilable artistic differences'. Bernardi's wife was left to express-mail the second of his two dress shoes after him.

had not looked at the work since conducting it five years ago in Santa Fe and did not even have time to get hold of a copy of the full score to refresh his memory on the flight. He arrived in London on 8 February, just three days before the General Rehearsal, leaving his wife to express-mail the second of his dress shoes that he had left unpacked in Canada.

The press release about Rozhdestvensky's departure cited 'irreconcilable artistic differences', but there had been an unfortunate slip. During a pressurized forty-minute telephone conversation with a *Daily Telegraph* journalist, Director of Marketing and Public Affairs Keith Cooper had let slip a description of Rozhdestvensky's conducting as 'like Massenet dressed up as Mahler'. The press were delighted to have a sound-bite, a peg on which to hang columns. The orchestra, in particular, was furious, seeing this flippancy as another illustration of how inappropriately the great men of music are treated by the management of the House.

On Monday, 14 February, it was freezing in London. Susan Graham sat in Make-Up with Ron Freeman, looking at a copy of a newspaper warning of snow. 'I've been on a diet,' she confided, adjusting her trousers, 'but ... it's all those fish and chips.'

It was busy in Make-Up, the wigged and pomaded men all needing pairs of cupid-bow lips. The on-stage quartet was filing into the Wings. 'It's the first time I've been visible and costumed,' whispered orchestra sub-leader Adrian Reed, one of the on-stage string players.

Chorister Beth Michael was extolling the virtues of her costume, designed by the woman who 'made Michelle Pfeiffer's costume for Catlady. It's comfy, easy to move in – I love it'. Several women with bare arms pulled their huge skirts up over their exposed shoulders to keep themselves warm as they waited backstage. 'They look marvellous when they're on stage,' hissed Jane Mitchell in her tall wig, 'because when they walk the ruffles on the skirt all go together. It looks like some sort of romantic glow.' Jane was one of the flying choristers, suspended above the Stage in a harness. 'It was terrifying to start with, but once we'd done it a couple of times I found it quite fun.'

Stage managers in their headsets hushed the wings. 'Quiet please, everyone.' Susan Graham straightened her waistcoat and britches. Mario Bernardi was ready in the Pit, the eyes of the orchestra upon him. 'He looks very calm, given the circumstances,' muttered a

OPPOSITE **C**affeine and nicotine
during the Interval of the First Night of *Chérubin*, overlooked by the chiselled features
of ballerina Dame Margot Fonteyn.

OVERLEAF **T**he wigs of the men in the Chorus
were no impediment to backstage calls home before curtain up.
It was a different matter for the women.

woman up in the Amphitheatre, who had clearly followed the newspaper coverage of Rozhdestvensky's abrupt departure. Nicholas Payne had settled down into his seat in the Auditorium.

From the first bar to last of Massenet's tripping score, the audience had been delighted: by the women flying above the Stage, by the sweeping wide skirts and 'camp' male outfits, by the stylized dancing, the exaggerated make-up and wigs, by Susan Graham's languid elegance. English dialogue had been written for the production, and eagle-eyed members of the audience identified the actress, Jane Gurnett, as Nurse Rachel Longworth from BBC1's *Casualty*. The evening was fun. The audience understood the *joie de vivre* of the opera and reacted to it. '*Chérubin* is a soufflé,' Nicholas Payne said, using another of his savoured culinary metaphors, 'something light, tasty, sparkling'.

Wednesday, 16 February, two mornings after the night before. London was still grey and cold. Nicholas Payne was at home having breakfast with his family. The First Night could not have gone better, but had it been to the taste of the critics? Mug of black coffee at the ready, he opened the papers to see if 'there is blood on the ice'. Next to a colour photo the size of a postage stamp, *The Times* headlined 'A Heady Taste of French Fizz', the *Independent* 'A Marriage Made in Heaven' next to a much larger picture. The review in the *Financial Times* was pretty good, too. For once, a production had been reviewed in the spirit in which it was meant. Nicholas Payne had another cup of coffee, for pleasure now not fortification, before setting off into the dirty, winter day to work.

At Covent Garden, the cleaners had been hard at it since seven o'clock in the morning. Jean Flower, Cleaning Supervisor, has worked at the House for thirteen years. There is a tradition for whole families to work at the Opera House – such as the Pursey family backstage – passing jobs down through the generations. Jean's husband is a carpenter, her daughter a cleaner up in the Amphitheatre and, until five years ago, her son-in-law was an electrician. (He now works at Guy's Hospital.)

The state of the Auditorium after the First Night of *Chérubin* was not too bad. 'With opera you get not high-brow, but people who somehow don't seem to make so much mess inside the theatre,' said Jean, 'but the ballet people ... When we have ballet you get more ice-creams sold and a lot of people don't eat them. So you go to pick up a carton and the

'It was terrifying to start with, but once we'd done it a couple of times I found it quite fun.' Contralto Jane (stage name Madeleine) Mitchell was one of the flying choristers in *Chérubin*, winched across the stage in a harness that left red strap marks on her bare shoulders. They were paid extra.

ice-cream goes flying across the floor.' Jean works until two o'clock most days of the week and alternate Saturdays. Her evenings belong to Bingo and the dog-racing.

'Mr Isaacs and his wife came with us to the Catford dog races,' Jean revealed cautiously. 'He fancied a dog and I said to him, it's got no chance – it hadn't won for about nine months. And the blasted thing went in at nine-to-one and he had a fiver on it.' Then, more seriously, she added: 'Some of them don't speak, because you're cleaners and they think they're a lot better than you. But he always speaks to everybody.'

Despite the huge amount of energy put into the publicity for *Chérubin* by Keith Cooper and his team, the 'bums-on-seats' press-and-rumour machine had been working very effectively on the lower-profile productions, too. Helen Anderson, Press Officer for The Royal Opera Company (as well as for the House itself) had ensured that Strauss's *Elektra* and Verdi's *Rigoletto* – both revivals – had nevertheless got their fair share of column inches. Even for a show that has been seen at the House many times, publicity is crucial. Every year there is potentially a new audience to reach, as well as those who want to know about a second or third opportunity to see something they have previously enjoyed.

Specifically-designed accessibility initiatives aside – from daily stand-by tickets and concessions to the Hamlyn Week in January and the Midland Bank Proms Week in May (which opened on 23 May with Rossini's *Mosè in Egitto*, the bald heads of many of the cast leaving some reviewers unable to resist *Star Trek* jokes) – one of the most effective ways to extend a nightly audience is to broadcast the sound nationwide to as wide an audience as possible. Tucked round the side of the House on the market side, by the staff car park, the BBC's outside broadcast (OB) van – with its distinctive BBC letters stamped across the side and its thick black trailing wires – is a familiar sight. Verdi's *Rigoletto* was just one of twelve operas that Season to get the Radio 3 treatment, and over a million people tuned in.

The orchestra used to be paid for each outside broadcast. These days, the musicians are given a lump-sum to cover an average of twelve live radio transmissions a year: sometimes there are more, sometimes less. Television payments are negotiated separately, although one minute of sound-and-picture and one minute of picture alone can be used for free.

Composed at the end of what Verdi called 'his galley years', the familiar chords of *Rigoletto* are light-years away from the abrasive harmonic language of the one-and-a-half hour *Elektra*. This production has been in the repertoire since December 1988, notable not least as one of the very few shows in the Royal Opera House where a woman – Sian Edwards – had been invited to conduct. The 1994 revival, by coincidence rather than design, followed suit. This time it was thirty-two-year-old Australian Simone Young, who had made her début with the Sydney Opera and had the distinction of being the first woman to conduct at a Viennese opera house.

It can be a long haul being a woman in any but the most obvious areas of the Opera House, from the bottom to the top of the building. The number of women working in the stage crew can be counted on the fingers of one hand. Dallas, another Australian, works up in the Flies. In this tough man's world, she admits it can be an isolating business, although she thinks most problems come from thoughtlessness rather than malice – 'You're a bunch of girls, is one term of abuse,' she grimaces – and confides that she has just taken down a picture of a Page 3 girl in the restroom up in the Flies. 'I wasn't offended, but it was a way of territorializing the workplace.' Then turning to put another heavy lead weight on to the ropes, she adds: 'I can give plenty of verbal back ... '

On Tuesday, 15 February, at the Grand Theatre, Blackpool, the Ballet Company was at the end of its three-city mini-tour, which had also taken in two dates in Leicester and two at the Corn Exchange in Cambridge. The snow from London had not worked its way up the country yet, but it was perishing cold in Blackpool. A poster announcing The Royal Ballet's *Dance Bites* programme had been stuck rather incongruously next to a big pink banner advertising THE NOLAN SISTERS. Inside, on the tiny raked stage, the Company's regular seventy-five minute morning class was in progress – the barres looked slightly precarious on the slope. Razzling out on the town last night had led to one or two casualties not yet making it in.

The contrast between Blackpool and Covent Garden could not have been more pronounced. Squashed into cold dressing rooms, with a malfunctioning coffee machine half way up the stairs and rails of costumes hanging up and down the narrow corridors, leg-warmers and fingerless gloves were out in force. There seemed to be electric kettles plugged into every power point of the small Blackpool theatre. Physiotherapist Aileen Kelly's equipment was wedged diagonally into a dressing room at the top of the building.

Curled up into sagging armchairs, some of the girls were making repairs to their shoes. Shoe Mistress of The Royal Ballet, Elaine Garlick, issues between ten and twenty pairs of pointes a month to each ballerina, depending on their workload, and these must last through classes, rehearsals and performances. Differences of toe shapes, the depth of the vamp (front), seven different weights of insole, foot widths, lengths, variations on the simple pink theme are endless: leather sole, silk satin-backed with calico, hard-fibre insole. The pointe itself is actually layer upon layer of flour-and-water paste, turned inside out and baked. Clear varnish is used to harden the pointe and protect it against sogginess. Each pair costs about £22.

After ten minutes, a new pointe starts to mould itself to the shape of its owner's foot. 'I can go into the dressing room, pick up a pointe and instantly recognize whose it is,' said Elaine Garlick. All sorts of techniques are used to give each pair a longer shelf-life: glue, spray with water or even saliva. At all levels of the ballet world, student to Principal, there is this routine, makeshift maintenance. By tradition, all dancers sew their own ribbons.

The matinée audience was at once very young and rather old – schoolchildren queuing up alongside old-age pensioners with discounted afternoon tickets. There was also a fair amount of rustling and sweet unwrapping, but as soon as the House lights dimmed the Auditorium shushed itself immediately.

Both of the two young choreographers whose work had been part of the opening programme of the Ballet Season had created new pieces for the tour. The curtain went up on William Tuckett's *Desirable Hostilities*, the black leotards a clear disappointment to some of the children who were expecting tutus. But they were excited by Matthew Hart's piece *Caught Dance,* a ferocious and agitated duet between Sarah Wildor and Tetsuya Kumakawa, a spider and her mate. The audience, attentive and inquisitive, responded spontaneously to the dancers' vigour and strength. Set to Lutoslawski's polymeric *Dance Preludes*, Matthew had dedicated the performance to the composer who had died just nine days before. But the children were less interested in this tribute than in trying to guess how high Tetsuya could jump: three metres (ten feet), six metres (twenty feet)? During the first interval, once ice-cream orders had been given, the chat was of little else. There was a very, very long queue for the Ladies ...

Ashley Page had choreographed the movement and dance for *Chérubin* seen in London the night before. Now it was the turn of the citizens of Blackpool to appreciate his work on Stravinsky's *Renard* in the second half. A fox, a cat, a wide-boy goat, the audience loved it, reacting enthusiastically and intelligently to the narrative and the violence of the chase. There was a lot of giggling at the first sight of Jonathan Howell's costume with its huge bright red penis, the cock protecting his six hens in their black tutus and yellow tights. And when Adam Cooper came on stage in *Herman Schmerman*, his yellow Versace skirt was greeted not with designer-conscious, but spontaneous, howls of laughter. (Of Deborah Bull, his partner on this occasion, a couple of women in the front row were heard to tut that: 'She could do with a bit of feeding up'.)

Several dancers reflected that the great thing about the tour was not only that they had all got to dance bigger roles than they would at home in Covent Garden, but that the audiences were so enthusiastic. As one ballerina put it, scraping out her yoghurt pot: 'When you're virtually sitting in their lap, it's nice if they let you know how much they're enjoying it'.

'I try and hit back at some of the lethal volleys

that come towards me, but I am not someone

who particularly wants to slug it out in open combat.'

Keith Cooper, Director of Public Affairs and Marketing

M A R C H

Keith Cooper and his press and marketing team had orchestrated a slick, serious publicity campaign to build up to the opening of Leoš Janáček's *Katya Kabanova* on Friday, 4 March. It was difficult to escape the opera: BBC radio discussed the history of *Katya Kabanova* and *The Storm*, the play by Ostrovsky on which it was based; commercial radio pondered the parallels between art and Janáček's life; director Trevor Nunn's distinctive face looked out from the covers of national newspapers over break-fast tables; there was the occasional reminder that the creative mind behind the sets and costumes belonged to Maria Bjørnson, the designer of *The Phantom of the Opera*; and glamorous colour photographs of Bernard Haitink filled the covers of music magazines, featuring a ret-rospective of his life and times. He would be spending his sixty-fifth birthday in the Orches-tra Pit conducting the first of *Katya*'s seven performances, and journalists were glad to have a peg to hang their articles on. (In this, the Press Office had found itself with competition – the team publicizing Dame Kiri Te Kanawa's televized fiftieth birthday concert at the Royal Albert Hall, six days later, was relying on the same strategy ...)

The publicity campaign for *Katya Kabanova* had not worked. Or rather, not enough people had been convinced that Janáček was for them. Jeremy Isaacs was worried. 'I am hoping for reviews and word-of-mouth that will have people battering at the doors to get in. But at the moment, as we open, we have an awful lot of seats to sell.' He admitted to always being twitchy at First Nights of new productions anyway, but the sheer frustration at the public's lack of taste – 'for a production that will be absolutely *brilliant*' – was aggravating at the very least. Even if the reviews were superb, his worry was that the gaps between the first and subsequent performances might not be enough to trigger the desperately-needed domino effect. Everybody involved – from stage crew to the singers, players and management – were proud of their achievement and disappointed by the number of faces in the Auditorium as they opened. The critics were all but unanimous. Lining up full-square behind the production, some voiced what many in the House were too diplomatic to say aloud: 'There was a depressing number of empty seats at the third performance of Janáček's *Katya Kabanova*,' wrote Rupert Christiansen in the *Spectator*, 'which only goes to show that rave reviews and true music drama don't necessarily cut much ice with the *lumpen* elements of public taste'.

There were some dissenting voices about the sixth revival of Otto Schenk's 1975 production of Verdi's *Un ballo in maschera* – a dull production and some rather flat singing – but on the whole the press continued to be kind for much of March.

On Wednesday, 9 March, many of The Royal Ballet's leading dancers were present at a Nureyev Gala at the Coliseum for the HIV/AIDS charity Crusaid. AIDS had killed Nureyev just over a year ago. At the last moment, Mikhail Baryshnikov pulled out citing other engagements. And the British press were gossiping about Sylvie Guillem – nicknamed 'Mademoiselle Non' – who was threatening to pull out too if the organizers did not let her choose her own material.

Classical ballet still likes its leading ladies traditional and compliant. 'Mademoiselle Non' does not fit this bill. Unusually tall for a dancer (1.75 metres – 5ft 8in – on the flat) with her sophisticated hennaed hair rather than the classical ballet bun, she inspires strong opinions: she's brilliant (arrogant, you mean); she's temperamental (spoilt); single-minded (rude). 'She could kill a man with one blow of her leg,' Jeremy Isaacs had once half-joked to a lunch of patrons and sponsors. Guillem was having a stormy Season. First her insistence in dancing *Herman Schmerman* in the *Winter Gala* in December, despite the fact the whole of the rest of the programme was inspired by Tchaikovsky. Then in January, during her first appearance

Darcey Bussell catching her breath.
It is only in the Wings that the Principals acknowledge the extreme
physical demands of their craft.

in Prokoviev's *Romeo and Juliet*, she had decided to expand her own interpretation of Juliet's suicide in the Final Act with the help of a blood capsule – without asking advice on how to use it properly. The rest of the cast and stage crew knew nothing of this until they were faced with Sylvie Guillem and an embarrassing splodge of red dye on the front of her costume. A bloody row broke out backstage as soon as the curtain came down and Deborah MacMillan – widow of Kenneth MacMillan who had choreographed the ballet – demanded an assurance that such an unprofessional thing would not happen again. Now, in March, the speculation as to whether or not Guillem would dance at the Nureyev Gala was made more poignant by that fact that she had been his protegée at the Paris Opéra Ballet. In 1989 the two had quarrelled violently over Guillem's contract. Storming out, she had arrived in England to offer herself as Principal Guest Artist to the delighted Royal Ballet. Even though she and her former mentor had been reconciled in the intervening years, Guillem had remained based in London.

The organizers of the Crusaid Gala were resolute. Guillem could not be the only performer to choose her material. As she had threatened, she pulled out and did not dance. But Darcey Bussell and Zoltán Solymosi and Irek Mukhamedov did, in the company of Natalia Makarova and Miss Piggy among others ... The newspapers, always interested in Guillem, loved the drama.

'Apparently,' Keith Cooper said with resignation, 'I was voted the most unpopular person in the organization in my earliest days here. I hope that was professional, rather than personal, but people just don't want to be changed.' He was finding it difficult to remember that he had actually been head-hunted by Covent Garden.

OPPOSITE 'I'm very intolerant of people
with their own agendas and I'm very intolerant of politics.' Keith Cooper,
Director of Public Affairs and Marketing, models a Paul Smith tie – a birthday present
from Michael Waldman and the BBC documentary film crew.

OVERLEAF Members of the cast watching Bussell at the
General Rehearsal of Tchaikovsky's *The Sleeping Beauty* in London in March 1994. Although The Royal
Ballet would not be heading West on its five-week American tour for another month, the set, props and
costumes had to be packed up and shipped off across the Atlantic to arrive in time for Easter.

Cooper's reputation is as a popularizer, a spin-doctor. But he is aware that his American-style attitudes to marketing are anathema to those within the organization who are more comfortable with the Chinese-whispers approach to publicity. 'It's like pushing spaghetti uphill,' he said urbanely. 'But I really see my role here as being part of moving it on. I am not ultimately going to be sitting here forever in the power and glory of the fund-raising supremo: that's for my successor.' Cooper had had to take a fair amount of friendly fire during February for his ill-guarded *faux pas* about conductor Rozhdestvensky and *Chérubin* – the 'Massenet dressed up as Mahler' comment – and even though he was now about to go into hospital for an operation on the base of his spine he had urgent staff problems to contend with.

Since Keith Cooper had taken up residence in December 1992, the Marketing Department itself had changed dramatically as the metaphorical new broom swept out the old. To opponents, even the modern designed offices in Bow Street are an outward and visible sign of the new order they dislike so much. On the walls in Keith's office hangs a framed poster for Verdi's *The Force of Destiny* ...

Back in January, Cooper had had an informal discussion with the Merchandising Manager, Kevin McDermott, about the future of the Royal Opera House shop. It had barely had time to recoup its start-up costs, but it was not proving as successful as had been hoped. The shop was a few yards up from the corner of James Street, the ear-marked home for The Royal Ballet in the development plans. Royal Opera House mugs, sweatshirts, place-mats, posters, videos of productions, recordings, histories and libretti filled the shelves. To Kevin McDermott, who had worked at the Royal Opera House for twelve years, the shop was the public face of the Opera House itself.

However, the decision had been taken to shut the shop. Kevin McDermott was told at the end of March that the new tenants would move in at the beginning of May. Disgusted, he handed in his resignation. Then, feeling that people had not been properly told what was going on, he posted his own explanation on Company noticeboards up and down the winding backstage corridors. There were low grumbles throughout the House at the unceremonious way the whole business apparently had been handled.

Decisions also had to be made about the Box Office. The antiquated telephone system, the butt of so many complaints over the years, was finally to be replaced with sophisticated state-of-the-art technology capable of coping with the House's thirteen-price schedules and 200 ticket prices, and its untold variations on the themes of standing, sitting and boxes. This overhaul of equipment would need to be matched by an overhaul in sales attitude and Cooper believed that current Box Office Manager Andrew Follon did not have the necessary skills.

Like Merchandising Manager Kevin McDermott, Andrew Follon was a long-term member of staff who had been promoted from Deputy to Box Office Manager at about the same time that Keith Cooper had arrived at the House. The problem would be to find a replacement for Follon with the requisite leadership qualities and relevant experience. There were very few comparable venues from which to poach: the South Bank, Barbican, Royal Albert Hall perhaps. Whoever the House attracted would also have to serve his or her notice before arriving in Covent Garden, which could leave an awkward interim period. When the axe finally fell on Andrew Follon in May, he felt he was a victim of the philosophy of change for change's sake. He was at once defiant and bitter. 'I saw a solicitor yesterday who told me that I have grounds for constructive dismissal, victimization and defamation of character,' he said, but then admitted that he did not really have the strength for a fight that could rumble on for years. A disillusioned man, he added as a parting shot: 'There are more performers off-stage than on stage.'

Even though *The Sleeping Beauty* was to open at the Kennedy Center in Washington, rather than at Covent Garden, a General Rehearsal had been scheduled at home at the beginning of March. The casts needed to try things out on stage in London before the set and costumes were shipped to America to await the Company's arrival on Easter Saturday. Because London would not be able to see the production until the following Season – November 1994 – security was tight for all stage rehearsals, the doors not just closed but metaphorically locked and bolted.

The day of the General Rehearsal was another bitterly cold day and both Anthony Dowell, Director of the Ballet, and designer Maria Bjørnson were prowling around the stage, testing the partially-constructed set as the stage crew continued to hammer. Was it all safe? The wicked fairy, Carabosse, was choreographed to be pulled out from under the enormous banqueting table in a small chariot by his three attendants. Derek Rencher – at sixty-one, one of the oldest members of the Company – was peering sceptically into the gloom. 'It's tiny,' protested the Queen, Elizabeth McGorian, reading his thoughts. She was wearing a black T-shirt with I'VE RIDDEN WITH THE VALKYRIES stamped across the front. 'Lose weight, lose weight,' joked Puss-in-Boots, Peter Abegglen. 'I'll have to have my legs cut off,'

OVERLEAF   'The set's everything the crew hates, really,' said the production manager for Janáček's *Katya Kabanova*. 'Metal, fibreglass, rubber. And parts of it are going to get wet.' Also designed by Maria Bjørnson, *Katya* opened in London a month before *Beauty* premièred in Washington.

retorted Derek. 'Have to have my false one shortened!' The Fairies looked ungainly on the Prologue staircase, their pointes clattering awkwardly down like wooden clogs on parquet. 'The boys will have to guide them,' mused Anthony to Maria. 'They can't see with their tutus.' Matthew Hart, one of Carabosse's rats, wanted to know if he could leap on the banqueting table and snatch something from the fruit bowl. 'If any of the boys do want to jump on it,' retorted Senior Stage Manager Keith Gray, 'then that will add another ten minutes to the start time.'

There was no audience, just empty A to Z rows as the men sprung high into the air, a monotonous thump, thump, thump as they landed. Tiny layered women – woollen leg-warmers and grunge T-shirts over their tutus – pirouetted and chasséed as the Stage Manager, Becky Hanson, reminded everyone that resin was *not* allowed on shoes.

'It's like an ice-rink,' muttered one of the more rebellious members of the Corps. 'We're all going to break our ankles.'

Anthony Dowell called the cast to order. 'Costumes-wise – for millions of reasons – we're tight, and it's incredibly tight technically. So you probably won't see some of the props until we get to Washington. Do the best you can.' He looked harassed. Maria Bjørnson – having seen *Katya Kabanova* safely up on time – looked determined.

In Washington, not only would the dancers have to get used to an entirely different stage, but to the strains of a different orchestra and the presence of 'rooky' extras, American actors and children auditioned almost on the day.

For the crew, too, it was a difficult situation. America has a more deregulated backstage environment controlled by strict working restrictions. In theory, the British crew would be at the Kennedy Center as advisers, helping their American counterparts, rather than running things as at the Royal Opera House. In practice there are many long-standing relationships between the House and Kennedy Center stagehands, traditions and productive working patterns which had been established over years of touring.

The decision about who goes on tour is a sensitive one. (In fact, the issue was set to become one of the trickiest sticking points of the BECTU negotiations as the Season grew older.) At a production meeting for the American tour, Assistant Technical Director John Seekings, Chief Electrician Paul Watson and Technical Manager Dave Reid were drawing up

One too many sequins?
Designer Maria Bjørnson (far left) and Darcey Bussell in one of her intricate costumes in Wardrobe. All together, there were eighteen costumes for the Principal ballerinas dancing Princess Aurora in Anthony Dowell's restaging of *The Sleeping Beauty.*

a final list. Quite a few people had put their names down and those not chosen would obviously be disappointed. There would be a contingent going out to Washington early to get everything ready for the First Night. Many of them would return to London the following day, leaving a small core to take the show to West Palm Beach, Austin, Houston and Orange County. Unreliability had discounted several people, inability to cope with the travelling or frequent sickness ruled out a few more. In the end, John Seekings estimated that there were probably only sixteen or seventeen stagehands who were serious contenders. 'You need people who not only achieve the technical side of the work ... but who are also good mixers and good communicators.'

The tour list was finalized, ready to be printed in the tour itineraries alongside hotel addresses, contact numbers and information about flights.

'On the whole, singers are very easy about money
in an emergency. They know if they are saving your show,
you are not going to be mean the next morning.'

Terri-Jayne Gray, Opera Company Manager

A P R I L

Gatwick South Terminal had rarely seen so many sleek, strong, beautiful, young people in one go. It was a damp cold Easter Saturday as one by one members of The Royal Ballet checked in for Continental Airlines Flight 25 to America. Irek Mukhamedov was travelling with his wife Masha and three-and-a-half year old daughter Sasha; Tracy Brown and her husband Christopher Saunders, both Soloists, had their ten-month-old son Peter with them as well as Chris's brother who would act as nanny during the five-week tour. But Fiona Chadwick, the first-cast Lilac Fairy, had left her young daughter Emily behind. Michael Nunn was there, too, saying goodbye to his girlfriend, Belinda Hatley, out of sight. She joined the group a little later, a little red-eyed. But the atmosphere was bubbly, buoyed up by excitement and a determination to have fun. Dancers weaved between holiday trolleys piled high with skis towards the departure lounge.

Peter Abegglen was having a quick cigarette before making his way down to the Departure Gate. A member of the Company for seven years, he grew up in Zurich and originally wanted to be a jazz dancer. When a friend told him that he should learn classical ballet technique first, he tried it, was good and auditioned for the Upper School in Baron's Court. A year later he was offered a place in the Company and has worked his way up through the ranks to Soloist. Like several of the male dancers, he was stylishly well dressed.

The Royal Ballet Company is an international one. There are dancers from Belgium, South Africa, Australia, Japan, France, Russia, Italy, New Zealand, Hungary, India and

Springtime in Washington:

two days before the world première of *The Sleeping Beauty* at the Kennedy Center,

Sir Robin Renwick – the British Ambassador – welcomes The Royal Ballet

to his official residence. Awaiting his cue is Jeremy Isaacs (right), with Michael Waldman (left)

and his BBC crew capturing the moment.

OPPOSITE S*tars and Stripes:*

the evening of Wednesday, 6 April 1994 – the Royal Gala and First Night – belongs

not to the dancers on Stage but to the security forces. A cast of thousands – the FBI,

the CIA, the Parks Police and sniffer dogs – were called in to protect not only Princess Margaret

but President Clinton and his family. Everyone entering and leaving the Stage area was frisked

and ballerinas were asked to pin their identity cards to their tutus ...

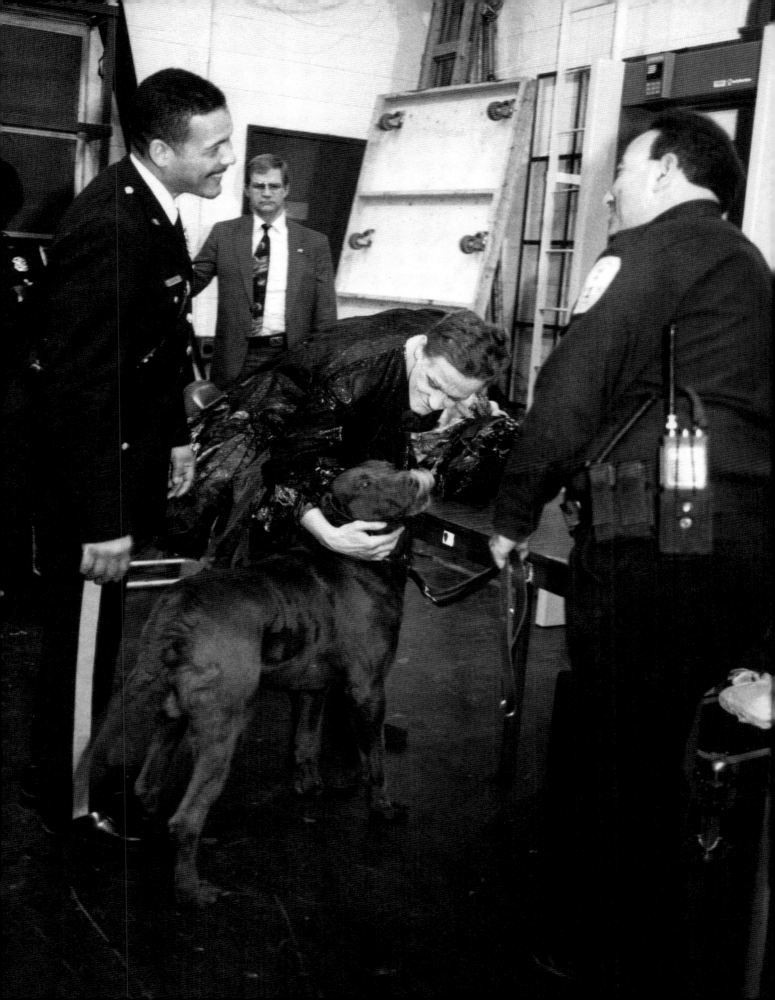

China, as well as from most corners of the British Isles. Peter is German-speaking Swiss and arrived in London with virtually no English. He communicated in French – the one language studied by all dancers – and taught himself to speak English by 'watching movies I already knew'.

The BBC documentary crew had been given permission to film on the plane itself, provided they did not get in anyone's way. 'Look, here's fluffy,' laughed one dancer as the sound recordist arrived with her boom mike. Adam Cooper was captured asleep with his mouth open and Irek Mukhamedov, seeing the camera pointed in his direction, smiled like a matinée idol causing half the civilian population of the plane to swoon. Some of the ballerinas took off their shoes and propped their stockinged feet up on the seats in front. With their legs perfectly straight, toes pointed, it looked like a row of donkeys' ears.

There was much hysteria over the visa waiver form, Section B of which asked: *Have you been arrested or convicted for an offense or crime involving moral turpitude … or are you seeking entry to engage in criminal or immoral activities?*

The hours passed.

The technical crew had taken an earlier flight. At that moment in Washington, early morning, scenery was being unloaded as seven lorries ferrying *Sleeping Beauty* paraphernalia and four carrying *Mayerling* and *Beatrix Potter* pulled up outside the Kennedy Center. The Stage Door and loading bays are at the front here, sandwiched between the two main entrances to the theatre, not tucked away out of sight.

'It's like unloading the QE2, isn't it,' joked Micky Berra, Head Carpenter and Union boss, in his thick New Jersey accent. 'Always good to do the best ballet company in the world.' Then seeing the look of sceptical indulgence on Anthony Dowell's face, insisted: 'Well, it's the truth, no question about it. We do them all, and you guys are the best.'

Assistant Technical Director John Seekings, Technical Manager Dave Reid and Ballet Press Officer Amanda Jones were in the wings. American and English stagehands were trying to force the *Beatrix Potter* basket – a huge piece of scenery – through the loading bay without having to dismantle it. Three metres (ten feet) up in the air, a bearded American was peering through the handle of the basket. On the back some wit had scribbled NEVER PUT ALL YOUR EGGS IN ONE BASKET. Grabbing a cigarette break, a clutch of stagehands were leaning against the cool, flat, exterior 1970s walls watching a woman in livid purple leggings power-walking round and round the Center. She reappeared every ten minutes, so became the clock by which the crew set their watches.

In the Kennedy Center the Wings are an eccentric and unofficial record of productions that have come and gone. Unlike Covent Garden, the Kennedy Center is a touring theatre and it is a tradition that each company leaves a memento: a makeshift poster reading ALL

THE WORLD'S A STAGE AND THIS IS THE BEST CREW; two huge jeep tyres; 4.5 metres (15ft) high Japanese lacquered walls. There is a basketball net high on the wall, with the NBL ball now wedged underneath a bit of scenery for *The Sleeping Beauty*. It is another tradition that the Covent Garden crew buys donuts for everyone on the first day. 'I didn't know that,' muttered Anthony Dowell.

Below stairs Senior Stage Manager, Keith Gray, was allocating dressing rooms. Like car-parking spaces for senior management, this is an issue that can turn lambs into wolves. A wicker hamper piled high with tutus was being wheeled along one of the corridors towards the lifts. Elaine Garlick, the Shoe Mistress, had brought ten-thousand pairs of shoes with her.

The next day, Sunday, was Easter Day, the only day of rest. Washington was beautiful, sunny, seventy-four degrees, white-and-pink cherry blossom trees everywhere. There was a queue outside the White House for the annual Easter Egg rolling on the presidential lawn. The dancers only had today to adjust, to unpack and prepare. Wednesday was not only the world première, but a Gala performance in the presence of their President HRH The Princess Margaret, and Bill, Hillary and Chelsea Clinton. Some tickets had been sold for a thousand dollars or more.

Each dancer is paid a tour allowance of forty-four dollars per day to cover food and drink as well as plasters, blister cream, aspirin, whatever. A steady stream of women and men were going empty-handed into Peoples Drug next to the hotel, and coming out balanced by carrier bags on either side.

Sisters Vanessa and Leana Palmer were sharing a room, for which they are ten dollars a day better off. Vanessa is a First Artist and has been with the Company for nearly five years, Leana for about two. Leana was stamping on a maroon, towel-wrapped all-in-one lycra outfit, apparently the only way to dry hand-washed clothes. It was a habit she acquired, her sister confided, on tour in Japan when the Company was without washing machines or driers for five weeks.

'All the girls are slim,' said Vanessa, 'although I don't think you would find one dancer satisfied with anything about himself or herself. There's always something that's wrong.' Leana is tiny, under forty-five kilos (seven stone). 'You're supposed to look vulnerable,' she added, slightly tongue-in-cheek. 'The poor things' backs can only take so much ... ' She was

OVERLEAF '**I** was waiting to come down the stairs
for my first entrance and I looked down at the other dancers and thought
if I just fall backwards, I won't have to go on.' Darcey Bussell and her Prince, Zoltán Solymosi, in the final
act of *The Sleeping Beauty*.

sitting with a bag of ice on her foot. The Corps often have to balance motionless for ages, legs going numb, then suddenly jump and land gracefully: injuries are easily acquired. 'Every available tart is what I seem to do,' commented Vanessa, cryptically.

On Tuesday, 5 April, there was a coiled-spring atmosphere backstage. The Piano Stage Rehearsal for tomorrow's opening night was scheduled to start at six-thirty. There is little excitement, just nerves and tension and defensiveness. Walking past, Head Carpenter Micky Berra stopped to tie up one of the bows on a drape. Some of the cobwebs had been packed too soon back in London said a twitchy Anthony Dowell, as he ungummed the sequins and net. The therapy value of this monotonous work had not gone unnoticed. 'I should take one out front on the first night and do it – sit and fiddle,' he added drily.

At six o'clock Dowell was on stage with Ballet Master Christopher Carr coaching the recently-acquired children and extras, all of whom were disappointingly graceless. The boys were mucking about, spinning on their heels. 'Do we have any sleigh drivers?' called Carr into the Auditorium. Legs leapt from a seat, charged through the red plush door and reported for duty moments later.

Drip by drip the dancers were appearing stage left. Most of the women were still in slippers or South American sandals, cardigans over their bare shoulders. Pushing their white-bandaged toes into their shoes, lacing up ribbons, they gathered round the gritty chalk box like chickens at a feed. Bent double from the waist, straight-legged, they poked and prodded their feet, then went up on their pointes to test the fit.

The first sight of the completed set was breathtaking. Sweeping arches and balustrades, the colour of bruises. No orchestra for this run-through. Tchaikovsky's generous melodies sounded comical in the cavernous space – a solitary pianist clutching at the notes of a score shrunk for only two hands. A few wobbles, the extras in the Prologue look bewildered. 'Can you put them in the right place,' yelled Christopher Carr, 'so they get it right ... '

The Royal Ballet made its American début at the Metropolitan Opera House in New York in 1949 with *The Sleeping Beauty*, the production with which Covent Garden had reopened its doors after the end of the Second World War. Margot Fonteyn danced Aurora, taking forty-seven curtain calls and being showered with enough flowers to fill the market back home in London. Over fifty years later it was the turn of Darcey Bussell, a classical dancer of talent and grace in a modern mould.

The daughter of a Fulham dentist, Darcey was plucked from the Corps of Sadlers' Wells and transferred to The Royal Ballet at the age of nineteen by Kenneth MacMillan to star in his ballet *The Prince of the Pagodas*. Now only twenty-five – four years younger than Guillem, two younger than Durante – Bussell is already an international *étoile* (as the Paris Opéra Ballet still calls its Principals), a rising celebrity. She is known for being nice. One of the most photographed ballerinas in the world – from Annie Leibovitz to *Vogue* fashion shoots – her legs were even voted by *Tatler* as one of the world's most perfect pairs; her portrait, by Allen Jones, hangs in the National Portrait Gallery; and her appearance in a BBC *French and Saunders* show – 'I taught her everything she knows,' twittered Mme French – secured her a popularity far beyond Covent Garden.

She is very tall for a prima ballerina – 1.7 metres (5ft 7in) – and famously lost the lead in The Royal Ballet's production of *Manon* for being too tall for Irek Mukhamedov. Zoltán Solymosi joined the Company from La Scala in 1992, his height, intemperate energy and flashes of brilliance the perfect balance for Bussell. He was to open as Prince Florimund.

As the General Rehearsal progressed, Darcey jogged – rather than danced – through her paces, the odd jump or pirouette linked with a chanted one-two-three walk for positioning and timing. The ivy-tendrilled wrought-iron gates – supposed to effortlessly glide shut when the Princess pricks her finger – nearly cut several of the sleeping court ladies in two. The technicians tried over and over again, sometimes too early, sometimes too late. Tempers began to fray.

By the beginning of Act III everyone was exhausted. Peter Abegglen and Larissa Bamber danced their Puss in Boots/White Cat duet, then launched straight into a post-mortem the instant they were back in the wings. Darcey Bussell's and Zoltán Solymosi's *Grand pas de deux* was not going well. Zoltán was in a world of his own, insensitive to anyone else's needs. The chant 'fucking shoes, fucking shoes' could be clearly heard on stage as he practised his jump over and over and over again in the Wings – thump, thump, thump. Darcey looked distressed. Anthony Dowell finally closed the irritable rehearsal after ten o'clock, packing off his cast for a good night's sleep. The Press Officer, Amanda Jones, looked exhausted.

At four o'clock tea-time on Wednesday, 6 April, three hours before the curtain was due to go up, the Parks Police arrived. Within an hour they had worked their way through most of the food in the canteen, their huge thighs and guns spilling off the chairs. Metal detectors were being put up at both entrances to the stage area. No one without a pass would be allowed through. No one. This was news to the cast and crew of The Royal Ballet. Muttering that he would end the week in a psychiatric clinic, Anthony Dowell was trying to explain that tutus do not have pockets ...

Next, the grey-suited Secret Police arrived. With wires running up the inside of their jackets to their ears, they were neat and inscrutable. Then the FBI. The building was now

OVERLEAF W hen London finally got its own
Royal Gala performance of *The Sleeping Beauty* in November 1994, it was Anthony Dowell,
Director of The Royal Ballet, who played the spindle-brandishing Carabosse.

surrounded. The arrival of four sniffer dogs was the trigger for the final security assault. 'Clear the area. The dogs are gonna sweep. Clear the area.' Administrative Director of the Ballet, Anthony Russell-Roberts did not have his pass, so was refused both entry and information by a ferocious woman in an ill-fitting black wig. 'When the dogs finish the sweep, that's when they finish the sweep,' she said. 'A'right.' It was past six o'clock. Never mind the ballet, the safety of the President of the United States of America was at stake ...

By seven o'clock, the senior crew was in evening dress rather than their usual backstage work clothes. Beginners had been called to the Wings. The atmosphere was nervous as dancers huddled round the mini-screen on stage right to watch the arrival of the Presidential party. A timpani roll, then the National Anthem was followed by the Star Spangled Banner which was followed by the Overture.

Darcey Bussell was looking terrified. 'I was waiting to come down the stairs for my first entrance – hanging off some bars with a three metre (10ft) drop behind me – and, as I looked down at the other dancers, I thought if I just fall backwards, I won't have to go on.' Throughout the performance Zoltán Solymosi's expression veered from preoccupied to tortured. He breathed increasingly heavily at every exit, sighing, scowling as he massaged his thighs in the Wings to keep the muscles working.

Suddenly the curtain had come down and *The Sleeping Beauty* was over. 'Where's me flowers?' hollered Senior Stage Manager Keith Gray, as Kennedy Center supremo Micky Berra nipped on stage ready to hold back the curtain for the individual calls. 'I'll take you on stage,' Anthony Dowell said to Maria Bjørnson, 'and we'll do a bow'. He looked ten years younger. Jeremy Isaacs and Tessa Blackstone, Chairman of the Ballet Board, tried to congratulate him as he turned to a sullen-faced Zoltán, nagging: 'We only saw your smile once.' 'Now we can *really* dance,' breathed Darcey as the Deathwatch photographers were herded behind a rope to await the arrival of President Clinton and Princess Margaret.

Somehow BBC director Michael Waldman succeeded in getting himself and his crew into the middle of the Stage, unrestrained by the red ropes holding back the rest of the press corps. 'What I need is a Lilac Fairy,' joked President Clinton, again under attack from sexual harassment-and-misdemeanours scandals. 'She would,' agreed Fiona Chadwick, 'guarantee you a happy ending.'

Covent Garden itself could have done with the ministrations of a Lilac Fairy, too. Discordant tones on- and off-stage marked the beginning of spring in London. The new Director of Personnel, Mike Morris had arrived, admitting, ten days into the job, that he was: 'finding it very tiring, much more tiring than I'd thought – the steep learning curve, there are so many new people to meet and to work out how they all fit in'. Charismatic, and thoughtful, he was not daunted by the scale of the task ahead and had already drawn the conclusion that the House didn't 'have a tradition of speaking openly'. He was horrified by the stage agreement. 'I have to say, that I regard the whole of the BECTU agreement as archaic. It's as if Thatcher had never happened.'

While trying to find his bearings, Mike Morris also needed to establish a productive working relationship with the senior management, particularly Jeremy Isaacs. He knew the Finance Director Clive Timms from ITN, but was yet to meet Keith Cooper, who was still recuperating at home from his back operation. 'It's essential to get on with the Chief Executive,' Mike stressed. 'It's essential – and it will grow with time.'

Nicholas Payne also had his hands full. Harrison Birtwistle's opera *Gawain* had been commissioned by the House and premièred at Covent Garden in May 1991. One of the most distinguished of living British composers – and composer-in-residence for the London Philharmonic – Birtwistle had none the less become the focus for many of the modernism versus traditionalism debates among classical music aficionados. *Gawain*'s angular and dissonant sounds had proved off-putting for many opera-goers more used to the cadences of Rossini and Mozart – 'hellishly difficult modern music', admitted Nicholas Payne. And because of its many impressive special effects, it was expensive to mount.

When budgets were being revised last year, *Gawain* had been a strong contender for axing. But by sleight of hand and passionate support from some quarters, not least Nicholas Payne himself, it had had a stay of execution and was finally inked-in for five performances during April.

It was not an opera much loved by the orchestra, even though fifteen minutes had been trimmed off its running time. String players – first and second violins, viola players, cellos and basses – sit two to a music stand, known as a desk. The closer you are to the conductor the higher your rank. Part of what makes an interpretation of a piece of music special is the decisions on bowing made by the conductor. Every single phrase, note even, is given a bow

OVERLEAF The Turning of the Seasons in Act I
of Harrison Birtwistle's *Gawain*. Birtwistle cut fifteen minutes from this part of the opera; in which night
follows day and season follows season until a year has passed:
cynics suggested that it was a decision more governed by financial than artistic considerations.

marking – **V** for up (starting at the point of the bow) $\prod$ for down (starting closest to one's hand) – which leads to the miracle of all bows of, say, the viola section, being drawn in the same direction at the same time. *Gawain* is an immensely densely-scored piece of music, with little instinctive bowing. The complexities of the beating, the time-changes in almost every bar, make it both unrewarding and difficult to play well.

The sheer number of notes and words in the score had led to an unusual decision after its first couple of performances in 1991. Surtitles were beamed high up above the proscenium arch that frames the Stage, despite the libretto being in English. Surtitles had first been used towards the end of Colin Davis's tenure as Music Director. 'Each cue is numbered,' explained Judy Mackerras, Surtitles Co-ordinator, 'so that the entire programme is pre-set. It is just a question of hitting a button.' But much like Head of Music David Syrus, squashed inside his Prompt Box, the Surtitles Co-ordinators have to be prepared just in case singers miss lines or radically alter pace. Occasionally, if something goes completely wrong, they have to project a blank while they search for the right caption. Adrian Reed, sub-leader of the orchestra, remembers surtitles having an immediate effect on audiences when first used. They started to react spontaneously to the narrative, able to follow the story in detail. And because the audience needed fewer visual signposts, directors could be more subtle.

Thursday, 14 April. Tickets for contemporary operas are notoriously difficult to sell. However, thanks to a free publicity campaign provided by a self-selected group of anti-Avant-Gardists – calling themselves the Hecklers – sales for tonight's performance had been healthy. The Hecklers had announced their intention to boo on the First Night, a declaration which had encouraged supporters of both Harrison Birtwistle in particular and the House in general to turn out in force.

Inside the Auditorium the house lights went down.

'Night after night/the same dream.' The words wound their way from Morgan le Fay, suspended in a fluorescent lilac circle above the Stage. Basing his opera on the medieval poem *Sir Gawain and the Green Knight,* Harrison Birtwistle had turned to poet David Harsent for his libretto for *Gawain.* The words are beautiful, powerful. The audience gasped at its first sight of the Green Knight, played by the great Wagnerian bass John Tomlinson, as he knocked at the door of King Arthur's winter court. François Le Roux was the eponymous anti-hero, painfully reluctant and unwilling. And young House Principal John Marsden was singing Ywain, his first named role.

Bass John Tomlinson as the Green Knight in *Gawain.* A cast was taken of Tomlinson's head and a mask designed by an off-shoot of the *Spitting Image* company. Both the eyes and the mouth moved.

L*e nozze di Figaro,*
Mozart's 'upstairs, downstairs' tale of eighteenth-century marital life. Twenty-eight-year-old
bass-baritone Bryn Terfel made his London début with English National Opera
as Figaro in 1991, singing half a mile down the road at ENO's Coliseum.

OPPOSITE The reluctant eponymous knight,
played by François le Roux, holding aloft the severed head of the Green Knight.
Commissioned by The Royal Opera, *Gawain* was premièred in 1991.

Gawain lifted his sword and decapitated the challenger. The shaggy green head fell. John Tomlinson bent down and picked up the head from the floor. It began to sing. A ripple went through the stalls as, one by one, the audience realized that the eyes were swivelling in the green face and the mouth was actually moving. (The green latex head, an exact replica of Tomlinson's face, had been made by an off-shoot company from *Spitting Image*.)

It is difficult music, nigh on impossible to catch hold of a melody, but *Gawain* is a fantastic visual feast and its rich colours, its marriage of the symbolic and the natural, make it a challenging theatrical experience. The opera ends, as it begins, with the soprano voice of Morgan Le Fay: 'Then with a single step your journey begins.'

Having behaved themselves during the entire opera, the Hecklers were now ready to boo. In the Orchestra Stalls, gang-leader Frederick Stocken stood up to heckle. Lord Gowrie – just into his first couple of weeks as Lord Palumbo's replacement as Chairman of the Arts Council – was one of the first to his feet, his cheers drowning out Frederick Stocken's petulant catcalls. It was somehow all rather English. Stocken, black-tied, politely standing in front of his expensive seat was ignored by everyone around him. Finally Birtwistle ambled on to take a bow, giving an amused victory sign to the enthusiastic Auditorium. A month later Sir Harrison was announced as the first professor of composition at King's College, London.

Outside the main entrance to the Royal Opera House, were Stocken's chums, one dressed as a vicar waving a thurible and carrying placard saying MODERNISM RIP. The *Newsnight* team was setting up monitors, intending to film a live exchange of views between composer George Benjamin and Frederick Stocken in the howling wind and numbing cold. Benjamin put the case for contemporary music, that audiences should be prepared to listen and involve themselves with things that did not seem immediately accessible. Stocken, his hands and nose frozen red, protested. 'It's self-denying music, it doesn't speak to the world.'

'I hope that the artists get the credit if it's a success,' said Nicholas Payne the following day, admitting that he had been stunned by the enthusiasm of the audience. His coffee percolator was spluttering furiously. 'I am prepared to take the blame if it is a failure.' He need not have worried, on the last night there was standing room only.

There was just one more Knight to come in April. First performed at Covent Garden in 1819 (in English), Mozart's *Le nozze di Figaro* was always a popular opera and bookings were looking fine for this third revival of Johannes Schaaf's 1987 production. The exuberant Welsh bass-baritone Bryn Terfel was singing Figaro, Jeffrey Black was Count Almaviva and Christine Brewer was making her House début as his Countess.

On Wednesday, 27 April, at ten past six, as the Crush Bar was already filling up, Terri-Jayne Gray had only just heard that Jeffrey Black would be unable to sing. An early curtain up, she had fifty minutes to find a replacement, a White Knight who not only knew the role itself but the House's production too, and could get to Covent Garden immediately.

The curtain was held. At five past seven, Terri-Jayne was standing at the Stage Door waiting for one of the House's most popular singers to arrive. Where, where, was he?

The saviour of the night, Thomas Allen had been singing in Los Angeles on Monday night and was still sufficiently jet-lagged to have agreed to chuck himself into a taxi and gallop across London. His black cab screeched down Floral Street. 'I need ten minutes,' he shouted as he belted through the glass Stage Door and charged down to the dressing room with Terri-Jayne in pursuit.

Jeremy Isaacs announced the unexpected cast change to the audience and apologized for the delay. 'I've always wanted to do that,' he said gleefully as he came off stage, 'go on and announce that Joe Bloggs couldn't sing, but his place was being taken by someone much better known.'

Thomas Allen – pulling himself into trousers and jacket, a quick splat of make-up – knew the production well having sung in both of its previous 'outings'. But he had never laid eyes on either tonight's conductor, Hartmut Haenchen, or his Countess wife. 'How tall is she?' he whispered *sotto voce* as he swept up into the Wings and on to the Stage. His first notes were drowned out by appreciative applause from the audience, enjoying this real-life drama being played out before their eyes.

'One down,' Allen joked cheekily to the stage crew in the Wings as the curtain fell at the end of Act I.

Newspaper billboards the following morning carried the inevitable headline 'Dramatic Rush Saves Opera'.

OVERLEAF 'The last major production of the 1993/94 opera season was well into rehearsal. Due to open in June, Verdi's *Aida* had a huge cast and over eighty extras – but no animals. American-born diva Cheryl Studer – Studer the Comet – sang *Aida*, but was taken ill just hours before the second performance and replaced by Nina Rautio. Next on stage was Russian soprano Galina Kalinina, after both the third and fourth Aidas had withdrawn before singing a note. Here the King of Egypt, Mark Beesley, is triumphant on the First Night, 16 June 1994.

'Any senior manager who is going to be any good is a politician,

because organizations are ultimately about people

and wherever you get more than two people together

you've got politics, haven't you?'

Mike Morris, Director of Personnel

M A Y

Mike Morris was sitting in his office with his deputy, Judith Vickers, Chief Electrician Paul Watson and Assistant Technical Director John Seekings, back from America and The Royal Ballet Tour. Morris was trying to get everything into some sort of context before his first negotiating meeting with BECTU in a couple of days' time.

As part of the drive to save money, the workforce had been told that action would be taken against those who were repeatedly off sick without just cause or persistently late. At first overtime would be withdrawn, then salaries would be docked. For Mike, this was just one obvious way of ensuring that public money was 'being wisely and efficiently used, and not being wasted'. The problem was that no one was sure when the system was supposed to have started. Judith was sure it had come into effect at the beginning of January, John thought it was the beginning of March. There would be a new grading structure as a result of the BECTU negotiations, but Mike Morris did not want to use this to deal with individuals who should actually be facing disciplinary action. He wanted all the loose ends tidied up before the regrading process started.

Mike, in fact, was becoming increasingly exasperated at the lack of organization. He took his glasses off, put them on again, a distinctive gesture. Management had put forward a proposal, union working parties had reported back, but exactly where had the proposals got to now? He wanted to announce a deadline of Friday 27 May for voluntary redundancies.

Judith had mounds of paper with her. Nobody seemed to know which wording for which clause was in which draft. There was also some confusion as to whether the conversations with BECTU to date had been discussions or actual negotiations. The meeting again veered off into self-justification. Two hours passed and little was achieved. 'The fundamental thinking hasn't been done,' Mike said afterwards to Judith. 'It just has *not* been done.'

Thursday, 5 May, and Pat Styles, Union Steward for the Nightgang, was not best pleased to be back in the House. 'I've been to work, gone home. I've fallen asleep in the bath for three-quarters of an hour. I've come to work for a nice meeting. That's life on the night crew.' He thought the whole negotiation process was little more than a PR exercise. 'You presume that the leadership will come from the senior management, because that's why they're paid lots of money. When that leadership is not forthcoming and you have a bit of a vacuum, you can't then be surprised when those on the ground say "sod that for a game of soldiers, I'm not playing", and don't show much initiative and interest.'

Today will be the first time that Mike Morris has met the BECTU negotiating team across the table. Both sides are apprehensive, but looking approachable. National BECTU official Gerry Morrissey is there as the supervisory officer for the Arts and Entertainment Division. A very capable man, Morrissey has predicted that the negotiations will take a year at least. 'Every time there's a gap between meetings there's nothing but disinformation going out,' he comments to Chief Steward Peter Coggon before the meeting starts. There is a slightly awkward shuffling of chairs as the management team arrives.

Mike Morris is slightly hesitant, as if he is embarrassed to be bringing up any of these issues at all. But he is direct as he puts the management's revised package on the table. There will be four project teams of twelve people – assigned to particular productions – plus a general running team to be called on as and when needed. Having listened to the union's reservations about multi-skilling, the management accepts that lighting board and follow-spots are a special case: each project team will therefore have its own specialists in this one area. Everyone else will be retrained to learn all the skills necessary for working on and around the Stage area.

That leaves twenty-four redundancies. Provided they are near that target figure, management will consider making up the full complement through natural wastage, retirement, and so on, over the next year or so. Management is also prepared to guarantee one three-day weekend every three weeks as compensation for the loss of the three-day week. On the grading structure, people will at first be moved straight across on to the new system: three months later there will be a wholesale review to iron out any miscarriages of justice.

Mike Morris lays his glasses on the table.

Gerry Morrissey immediately asks for an adjournment. BECTU stays put. Mike Morris

Two of the three tenors were at
the Royal Opera House during the Season. José Carreras was never too busy to sign autographs
before and after rehearsals for *Fedora*. Having grown a Clark Gable moustache for his part in a Revue,
Stage Door keeper and amateur singer Sandy Kennedy keeps an eye on the LP-waving crowd.

and his team remove themselves to another room along the corridor. The sound of the orchestra can be faintly heard over the tannoy: a major key, sounding happy.

Peter Coggon rolls himself another cigarette. Management has not moved much, summarizes Gerry. It has increased basic salaries, sure, but because of the loss of overtime pay most people will be financially worse off under the new system. He does not feel this is enough to warrant acceptance of the package. 'Because this is a working party – rather than a negotiating committee – we'll have to go back to the members before responding,' says Morrissey. Mike Morris looks astounded as Morrissey warns that management must not put out a call for voluntary redundancies until agreement has been reached … The House grapevine being what it is, twelve letters or so have already been received – including a couple for people who Assistant Technical Director John Seekings would rather not lose.

In his calm unflustered way, Mike is furious: 'You ask for endless, endless clarification,' he says, taking off his glasses again, 'yet there is no feedback.'

The fourth tenor?
As crowds in the piazza wait for the Big Screen Relay
of Denyce Graves and Plácido Domingo in *Carmen* on 20 May 1994,
a policeman removes a less-than-tuneful fan.

Peter Coggon is depressed by the meeting. 'I'm thinking of retiring early – today anyway. I don't think it'll be a very fun place to work. It will be too big a loss of earnings for people who've worked here for years and disrupt a lot of lives.'

'Ladies and gentlemen of the Chorus to the Opera Rehearsal room,' calls the tannoy. 'Thank you.' In the canteen, women and men drain their coffee cups, stub out cigarettes, then gather up handbags and scores and jackets from the backs of chairs to make their way back. 'Act II beginners for *Fedora* to the Stage, please.' Then, after a pause: 'Ladies and gentlemen and music staff please disregard that last call. We won't be starting until half-past twelve. Thank you.' Silence.

Giordano's end-of-the-century opera, *Fedora*, was premièred in 1898. Based on Sardou's first melodrama for the great Sarah Bernhardt, a certain amount of musical snobbery surrounds the opera – the poor person's *Tosca*, according to some – and it has not been performed at Covent Garden since June 1925. This production had been prèmiered triumphantly at La Scala in Milan in 1993, a showcase for Italian diva Mirella Freni partnered alternately by Plácido Domingo and José Carreras. Now Associate Music Director Sir Edward Downes, in his forty-second season at the House, is to conduct Freni and Carreras.

'People seem very suspicious that it's musical lemonade,' Ted Downes expanded, 'but Giordano wrote extremely well for the voice. The music expresses full-blooded passions that hit you in the gut. The orchestra didn't know what to expect, but, at the end of the first rehearsal, I saw all these beatific smiles and they were all singing and humming tunes.'

The press has been running a relatively low-key campaign for several months against the huge fees paid to the very top operatic stars who, in its opinion, are past their sell-by dates. There are also press rumours of stadia concerts being cancelled for lack of interest, of tenors who are now unable to control their higher registers.

Mirella Freni is nearly sixty. She made her Covent Garden début thirty-three years ago. José Carreras – one of the three tenors taken to the hearts of millions of football fans after Italia 90 – first appeared over twenty years ago. But, in many ways, the issue is snobbery not quality. A few journalists seem offended by the popularizing of opera and the 'undiscriminating public' who pay huge sums to see – rather than listen to – the megastars.

The public, however, does not care about the critics' carping, not at all. Whenever rumour spreads that these two 'legends' are in the building, queues spring up from the Stage Door all the way down Floral Street.

Six performances of *Fedora* are scheduled – one of which is to be big-screen relayed live to the Covent Garden piazza and broadcast by BBC Radio 3 – and every performance is already sold out. Peter Meade, the Head Stage Door Keeper, is delighted to welcome José Carreras back to the House. 'He is charming,' he says. 'He comes in the door and always says, "*you*, don't give me any trouble," just for a laugh and a joke.'

The General Rehearsal on Friday, 6 May, was originally going to be closed to the public, but at the last moment it is decided to let in members of The Friends. Security is tight though. All the front rows in the Stalls Circle are cordoned off. Here and there, the odd A4 sheet with KEEP ROW CLEAR has been stuck to the underside of a seat. Only House personnel and ten press photographers are allowed in the Orchestra Stalls. Nicki Spencer, Deputy House Manager, slides through the closed red curtains: 'Please remember that this is a working rehearsal, not a performance. Some performers may not be singing out.'

The lights go down and there is the legendary Mirella Freni, plumping up cushions in a St Petersburg parlour. The photographers let fly a battery of shutters. As José Carreras makes his first entrance, the music ripped by yet another volley of quick snapping, a woman hisses to her friend: 'He's shorter than you think'. The first duet is wildly applauded, and their second, and their third. As the strains of the famous Act II aria *Amor ti vieta* die away the audience response is so exaggerated that Caruso himself might have blushed. There is a constant staccato, hands and shutters, hands and shutters.

For the big-screen relay on Thursday, 19 May, part of the BOC Covent Garden Festival, fans from all over the country come to hear this one, free open-air broadcast of *Fedora*.

The big screen has been erected along the side of the House in the piazza, next to the Floral Hall. Crumpled red Royal Opera House banners run down either side and across the top. On the small plain stage stand three rather forlorn-looking microphones.

THE WAY FORWARD – REBUILDING THE ROYAL OPERA HOUSE proclaims the on-screen title. At six o'clock the second of two promotional videos is showing. Jeremy Isaacs's voice fills the piazza: 'We want a bigger and wider audience to enjoy performances such as this'. Then Bamber Gascoigne – 'University Challenge?' giggles an elderly woman to her neighbour – presents a short film about the Dickensian working conditions backstage and why the redevelopment of the Opera House site is so important. Technical Director John Harrison, Nicholas Payne, *Meistersinger* and *Mitridate* director Graham Vick, baritone Thomas Allen – always good in a crisis – perform earnestly for the cause.

It is an effective piece of PR, but it is a grey evening, and a little cold. Young and old, the crowd is mixed, although there are clearly more opera die-hards than uninitiates just passing through the market. Is it a different audience from the one taking its seats inside the Auditorium? Perhaps. There are fold-away chairs, blankets, picnics ranging from home-made tuna pasta and red wine to baked potatoes and half a pint from the cafés nearby.

At six-thirty there are new arrivals. Women and men in pink sashes enter the piazza carrying shiny silver-and-red balloons with FREE PROGRAMMES stretched across them. Members of the Covent Garden Community Association are trying to drum up support for its petition against the Development. Some younger people listen, take leaflets, but several – including two women who are members of The Friends of Covent Garden anyway – are offended to be approached. The Association has a page in the programme, too, a brief resumé of their twenty-three year history which does not mention its long-running battle with the Opera House. There are a few barriers for crowd-control, but the police do not look as if they are expecting any problems.

The reviews after the First Night of *Fedora* had been polite. But every night inside the Auditorium, the curtain calls were accompanied by hundreds of flowers, daffodils thrown down on to the stage for the flunkeys to gather up. Clumps of autograph-hunting fans gathered at the stage door, kept in check by Peter Meade and his team.

When the live relay finishes, Mirella Freni and José Carreras reward the loyalty of their *al fresco* fans. Muffled up against the chill air, they make their way to the tiny outside stage. 'Did you enjoy it?' asks Carreras. 'Yes,' thousands of voices chorus back. 'Well, I will believe you and not the critics ...' he responds happily.

On the following day, Friday, 20 May, the screen relays Denyce Graves and Plácido Domingo in *Carmen*. (The production had come back in April with Jacques Delacôte conducting.) In a shower of publicity, Domingo has arrived to sing Don José for the last few performances, twenty-one years after his role début at Covent Garden.

'When Covent Garden wheels out ageing stars, expect a rip-off,' advised the *Sunday Times*, 'but see Domingo in *Carmen*, even if you have to stand.'

Nearly 7000 people are standing in the piazza for this special last night, compensated yet further by Angela Gheorghiu singing Michaela at short notice. Inside, some seats had sold for over £200, figures denounced by the critics. 'Interestingly,' Keith Cooper points out, 'after the £267-ticket scandal was "revealed" by the media, the Box Office was jammed with people trying to buy £267 seats – so we must be doing something right ...'

Friday night is even greyer, even colder. A firework display after the opera has been organized by the Covent Garden Community Association as the climax to the week's Festival. But half-an-hour before the end, torrential rain starts to beat a tattoo on the cobblestones of Covent Garden piazza. No one moves. Inside, Denyce Graves is presented with armfuls of flowers gathered up by the Flunkeys, the disappointments of January and her lost voice long forgotten. With Plácido Domingo, she processes through the rain to greet their stoical, resilient fans. Covered in what looks like tarpaulin, Domingo pats his throat to apologize for not singing live to them. Fireworks start chaotically to explode around him and his Carmen as Jeremy Isaacs rushes up saying: 'Hold the fireworks!'. The drenched crowd loves it.

'One season there was a party in the Crush Bar, to which everybody was invited,' reminisces Peter Meade at the Stage Door. 'About two-thirty I wandered downstairs to get my coat, the place in darkness. Suddenly a figure loomed up behind me and it was Plácido, still in his full outfit. And he said, "Are they still waiting out there? What shall I do?" We opened up, turned on the lights and he started singing. He did an extra performance for them.'

Mike Morris has spent the previous few days trying to be upbeat and positive, despite slightly belligerent looks all around him. The second of a three-day series of negotiation meetings, vision versus detail is the order of the day so far. He and Gerry Morrissey have got bogged down on whether the average new Grade 4 salary would be higher than its current equivalent: Mike says it will, Gerry says it won't. The union is voicing its fears, too, about those not selected to be in one of the project teams. 'I am a second-class citizen of the Royal Opera House because I'm doing nothing more than general humping,' is how Gerry insists those in the pool will feel.

In the end it comes down to money. Mike feels that if they could reach agreement on this, then it will be easier to negotiate on other issues. There is the old management/union divide: management thinks people should prove they are capable of doing a job *before* being appointed, the union vice versa. Throughout the meeting Mike Morris takes off his glasses, puts them on again; off, on. Gerry Morrissey taps away on his calculator. Peter Coggon rolls a cigarette. An adjournment sees both sides accepting they have reached an impasse, negotiations have broken down. 'I'm sorry, but there it is,' says Morris.

In a way, the management team is the more surprised, the more disappointed and its post-mortem is depressing. John Seekings is convinced that if only they could by-pass the union negotiators and talk directly to the workforce, agreement will be forthcoming. Mike Morris, with years of experience behind him, knows that the negotiators themselves are usually less militant than those they represent. He can see little alternative other than to go into dispute. His predecessor, Richard Wright, had always thought that they would end up at the arbitration and conciliation service ACAS, confides Judith Vickers. 'What killed the agreement for me,' explains Morris, 'was my sudden fear of losing the savings.'

Wednesday, 18 May. Peter Coggon comes out of his flat in Pimlico and sets off for work on his motorbike. A stone's throw away, Mike Morris closes the front door and gets into his car. He is going to have to face Jeremy Isaacs this morning. It will not be a comfortable meeting. 'We are about £1000 a man apart in payment,' is Morris's opening gambit as a car alarm wails in the street outside. 'We have two stark choices. Either we get a negotiated settlement or we don't – there's no other route.'

Dismissed, Mike Morris picks up the phone to ring Gerry Morrissey at BECTU's headquarters in Wardour Street. 'Hallo, theatre division. Hallo? Hallo?' A fault on the line. The voice at the other end cannot hear Mike. It is a moment of pure, unconcious theatre. Five minutes later, the two men are connected and agree that they might be able to shuffle closer to one another in a scaled-down informal meeting.

As Peter Coggon says: 'It's hard going really, like I was saying, democracy in action. It takes forever!'

'From time to time, members of the public book boxes because they are secluded and away from the rest of the audience. And they get up to mischief ... let's put it that way.'

Ivell Arnold, Commissionaire/Manager

J U N E

After a freezing-cold Easter and wet-and-miserable early summer, London was now in the grip of a heatwave. 'No one can breathe,' said Opera Company Manager Terri-Jayne Gray. 'The singers are very anti air-conditioning because it dries out the cords.'

Thursday, 16 June, was the First Night of *Aida*, the last new opera production of the Season. The temperature in the Pit was approaching twenty-eight degrees. In the Auditorium, the audience was moaning about the lack of air-conditioning. The higher up in the building you sit, the worse it gets. Verdi's four-act opera had been premièred in the ferocious heat of Cairo towards the close of the nineteenth century, so the atmosphere in the House that night was appropriate. Some one-hundred years later, this production at Covent Garden was even being sponsored by the Peninsular and Oriental Steam Navigation Company. But most of the women and men in the House were more interested in fanning the humid air with their programmes than in historical precedence.

The critics were out in force, rubbing shoulders with a First-Night crowd which included the Majors, the Heseltines and the Gowries. As the short Prelude finished and the curtain rose to reveal Ancient Egypt preparing to fight the Ethiopians, a belligerent woman in the Orchestra Stalls whispered ostentatiously to her neighbour, 'they look like Texans ...' In the pause between Acts I and II some twenty minutes later, a couple of people tried to escape for some fresh air. And a flustered man in the Amphitheatre – with imminent World

Cup football clearly on his mind – muttered that he had never before noticed the similarity between Verdi's Triumphal March and the Argentinian National Anthem ...

'Have you seen the opening?' asked Jane. 'What's it like?'

'Smoky,' replied Beth dryly.

'Oh.'

Chorus members Jane Mitchell and Beth Michael were not due on stage until seven-forty-five. They were contemplating their careers. 'I think that if I was going to rise to very lofty heights as a Principal,' said Jane meditatively, 'then that would have started to happen already. I feel that it's pointless hoping for very large roles in Class A Opera Houses ... so I'm actually aiming at something a little lower. I want to be a working singer – it's very important to me to be working – and people who do smaller roles tend to have much longer careers because they can do those roles in closer succession than if they are doing very large ones.' Jane is a contralto. She wants to move on from the Chorus of the Royal Opera House – somewhere like the Opera Studio would be perfect – but does not think that her vocal technique is up to auditioning. Ironically, everything else – acting, experience, confidence – is in place. 'It's almost like having the right ingredients to make a cake,' she says, 'but not having the right recipe'. Beth, a soprano, is more optimistic. She feels that she has reached the age when her voice is just starting to come into its own. 'I don't want to still be here in the Chorus when your programme goes out,' she told BBC television documentary director Michael Waldman.

They turned to contemplating *Aida* instead. Neither Jane nor Beth thought that the production was quite what the public wanted, despite the huge cast and around eighty extras. 'No animals,' said Jane by way of explanation. 'I think they want to imagine *Ben Hur* on stage.' A long and complicated call crackled over the tannoy.

'My particular favourite call is 'actors with judo-tops and warrior-bottoms', laughed Beth, adding: 'Do you know there's one woman in the chorus who always pinches the bottom of one of the male acrobats – on stage. I don't think she realizes that he's not interested in ladies ...' They both tugged at their 'jingle-bell costumes,' and adjusted their veils and head-dresses. 'They're not awfully comfortable in this heat,' said Jane between tugs. 'Pink, orange, green, we look like Smarties. But I presume we look good from a distance.' Beth raised her eyebrows. The tannoy called them. 'At least in Verdi the chorus has a good chance of a good yell,' Beth muttered as they set off for the Wings.

Covent Garden needed an outstanding *Aida*. Twice before the Royal Opera House had tried. On the second occasion, the celebrated partnership of Katia Ricciarelli as the Ethiopian slave girl Aida and Luciano Pavarotti as her Egyptian lover had even been booed. A production that should have been a mainstay investment for the future had been consigned

A priest-extra for Verdi's *Aida*
warming up backstage, observed by a covered harp and the portable conductor's rostrum,
used when there is an offstage band.

to the dustbin. Now, ten years on, the established Verdi team of designer Michael Yeargan and director Elijah Moshinsky had been commissioned to make it third-time lucky.

In the days leading up to the opening night there had been much talk in the papers about the curse of *Aida* at Covent Garden. Moshinsky had been interviewed. 'People don't take *Aida* seriously at the moment,' he had said. 'They consider it a Wembley opera,' he had added protectively. 'But what it offers is a complex pre-Marxist view of history as an endless power struggle inside which individual moments of conscience are possible.'

Three sopranos were to sing Aida, including American-born diva Cheryl Studer. Dubbed 'Studer the Comet', she had made her name as a Wagnerian soprano and had a reputation as someone who had appeared from nowhere overnight. Thursday, 16 June, was not only her first appearance at Covent Garden in six years but surprisingly – for a woman who had made a staggering twenty-eight complete recordings in ten years of a range of roles rarely tackled by the same singer – it was also her début in the role. She described *Aida* as a *Mordstück*, a killer piece.

As Cheryl Studer took her curtain calls at the end of the First Night, the cheers and applause were interrupted by a persistent booing from the vicinity of the Stalls Circle. She ignored them. The Flunkeys brought on her bouquets and, weighed down by flowers, she mouthed 'thank you, thank you' with great composure. 'I'm used to it,' she shrugged later. 'There's a group of people who follow me around, a kind of anti-faction.'

The critics – while in the main deploring the rudeness of Studer's reception – were, by and large, unimpressed with the production. It had certainly not banished the curse of Royal Opera House *Aida*s. 'I blame the weather,' wrote Rupert Christiansen in the *Spectator.*

'There's normally one a season that's dogged by illness,' sighed Terri-Jayne Gray, 'and this year it's *Aida*. Usually, however, it's a winter show, when everyone has flu and colds and things.' In the hot weeks that followed, casts were shuffled in and out of roles with alarming regularity. The House had lost its Amonasro – Aida's father and King of Ethiopia – before the production had even opened: Justino Diaz had been flown in from New York at the last moment to take Alexandru Agache's place. Cheryl Studer was taken ill just hours before the second performance: the Russian soprano Nina Rautio – whose début in Verdi's *Un ballo in maschera* had been encouragingly reviewed back in March – stepped in, due to sing the role in any case a few performances later. But the curtain still went up late (much to the delight of the ladies and gentlemen of the orchestra and chorus who had had precious few overtime payments during the Season due to management's improved housekeeping). The third Aida, Hungarian soprano Julia Varady, had to withdraw. So did *her* replacement Sharon Sweet, leaving the stage clear for Galina Kalinina to enjoy a spectacular success. Welsh tenor, Dennis O'Neill opened as Radamès, followed by Michael Sylvester: then Sylvester's back went, letting in Icelandic tenor Kristjan Johannsson to entertain the thousands of spectators at the open-air big-screen relay in Covent Garden piazza a few weeks later. Not one performance was cancelled. 'We've only lost one performance since the War,' boasted Terri-Jayne, 'and that was postponed rather than cancelled ...'

Perhaps it was the heat that encouraged mischief in the Grand Tier? Perhaps it was the production itself that led to the audience being riveted by the people in Box 38 rather than by those they had paid to see? Commissionaire/Manager Ivell Arnold was not prepared to speculate, as he told television director Michael Waldman about the level of sexual activity that occasionally went on during performances. 'It goes on in all productions – not just one particular production – although they have more time in Wagner, let's put it that way!' Elaborating, Ivell said: 'We had a situation the other night where all eyes were turned on this Box – not the stage – and come the interval I had had numerous complaints and had to go and

Sir Edward Downes, Associate Music Director,
waiting to go into the Orchestra Pit to conduct. Claustrophobic and low-ceilinged, the area is crowded
with double bass cases, old scores, music stands and school filing cabinets. Just round the corner
is the imposing Stage machinery, powered by First World War submarine engines.

investigate what was happening.' Warming to his theme, he continued: 'Well, I tapped on the door – because I could tell they were still in there – and a few minutes went by and nobody answered. I kept tapping and eventually the door opened. I was expecting to see somebody at face level, but this person was literally on the floor – I could just catch sight of a lady's face on the floor. And she said "Yes?" And I said, "Excuse me, Madam, I am afraid you *must* be seated in the box". And the door slammed. Eventually, after a minute or two, it opened again and a patron I recognized came out. And he said, "I realize that we shouldn't be doing this in the Boxes, but that's what I thought they were for!" And I said, "Unfortunately, they are not – and it has been noticed by members of the public," and could you behave, as it were. It was quite embarrassing at the time,' Ivell added, 'although the patron thought it was quite funny. But it's all part-and-parcel of dealing with the public.'

Later, when he was once again being interviewed by Michael Waldman – this time in his tiny office surrounded by spare commissionaires' uniforms, daily rosters and postcards from staff who had now moved on – Ivell told of another incident which had occurred a couple of weeks earlier in the Crush Bar. This had been even more public than the antics in Box 38. 'After the interval,' Ivell began, 'I have to shout out "Ladies and gentlemen, please return to your seats as the next Act is about to begin".' (It was another very hot night.) 'Most of the foyer was clear and I had just walked over to the stairs when I noticed there were a lot of flash-lights in the mirror at the top of the stairs. So I went upstairs and there were about fifty gentlemen surrounding the Crush Bar doors. As I got closer I could see that there was a top-less lady having her photograph taken by her friend or boyfriend or whoever, and she hadn't a care in the world. She was posing in all positions, you know, and I thought what do I say? So I said, "I'm awfully sorry, but photography is not allowed". And all the men shouted out "Spoilsport!" By this time, the lights were going down in the Auditorium and they just ran in. The topless lady, however, put her blouse on and came and sat in the foyer until the next Act commenced. Then she went in and watched the show.'

Ivell – who is part of security at the Stage Door during the day – continued to tidy up his tiny office. 'This is not an office really,' he said emphatically, 'it's the smallest changing room – considering what I have to keep in here. Then again, the House has lack of space everywhere for people, that's why we need a new opera house.' As a parting shot to the film crew, he repeated: 'A *big* opera house with *more* rooms and changing rooms et cetera ... get some more money for that!'

In this, the Royal Opera House was trying very hard – not only to get more money but to firm up the timetable for the major redevelopment of the Covent Garden site once and for all. The Development Project was due back before Westminster City Council at the end of June to hear whether or not it was to be granted planning permission for the Phase II Development.

The revised plans for Phase II were supposed to have gone before Westminster City Council on 14 April, three weeks before the local elections. Leading up to Easter, there had been a concentrated spat of pro- and anti-Development articles in the national and local press, exactly the time when Director of Public Affairs and Marketing Keith Cooper had been away on sick leave. The Theatres' Trust had made known its support for the House's revised plans. 'It is greatly to be hoped,' its Chairman had said, 'that this scheme can be fully funded and completed within a reasonable time.' The Covent Garden Community Associ-ation, on the other hand, was as opposed as ever to the Development programme and had accused the House of trying to bulldoze the plans through the planning process – a view shared by Westminster Council Opposition councillors. 'To be frank,' said Labour's Steve Hilditch, 'I smell a rat when a development the size of this is rushed through committee immediately before the council elections.'

It was against this backdrop that Sir Kit McMahon, Chairman of the Development

Board – and member of the Main Board – had accepted an invitation to attend a Community Association meeting at the beginning of April to present the revised plans in detail. With him on the platform were Dick Ensor, Chief Executive of the Development Project, and architect Jeremy Dixon, one half of the Dixon Jones partnership responsible for the inspirational new Henry Moore museum in Sheffield.

The atmosphere was combative. Sir Kit McMahon outlined the changes they had made to the 1990 plans, such as the reduction in the height of the Fly tower and the junking of the office-block scheme. But the battle-lines were too entrenched for his words to be persuasive. The Covent Garden Community Association was furious that the House was being allowed to take its plans back to Westminster in a fraction of the usual time needed for major planning projects. It even threatened to take legal action against the Council if it approved designs that turned out to be insufficiently detailed. Like the Arts Council – who had hauled Jeremy Isaacs and the Development team over the coals during their Joint Action Committee meeting in February – the Association wanted to know who was going to foot the bill. 'You're continually warping the facts about the cost of this scheme,' shouted a voice from the floor. 'The Opera House is like a caricature,' insisted Jim Monahan, an architect himself and Chair of the Community Association. 'It's like a merry-go-round. If you're not on one committee, you're on another.' The publican of the Marquis of Angelsey – a popular performers' haunt, in Bow Street, a hundred yards down from the main entrance to the Opera House – accused the platform of giving no thought to the fact that, under the new designs, he would be expected to endure lorries loading and unloading right opposite his bedroom window at all times of the day and night. 'It's totally élitist,' raged Jim Monahan. 'You continue to run it in an élitist way and the whole design shows it.'

Tempers were barely controlled, the criticisms honed by years of practice. In the event, the plans were not ready by 14 April and the local elections came and went before the revised plans were considered by Westminster City Council. The Tories had retained control. On the night, the Council hedged its bets. It agreed that the amended proposals were 'a substantial improvement on the 1990 scheme', thus, in a sense, giving its blessing. But, at the same time, it deferred the final decision until the end of June. It wanted clarification of information about safeguarding the storage and relocation of the Floral Hall; it wanted more elevational details; it wanted more detailed plans about access for the disabled; and it wanted to know more about 'greening initiatives' and public conveniences ... The list went on.

From the cramped Wings,
Principal Adam Cooper and First Soloist Nicola Tranah
watch their colleagues in *Danses concertantes*.

Scheduling takes no account of the weather.
Winter Dreams is set in a nineteenth-century frozen provincial Russian town and the dancers
are costumed in heavy uniforms, cloaks and furs. In the Wings in twentieth-century London
in a heatwave, Irek Mukhamedov tries to wipe away the sweat with a paper tissue.
Kenneth MacMillan choreographed the role of Vershinin for him.

Nevertheless, Kit McMahon, Jeremy Isaacs and everyone else concerned allowed themselves a collective sigh of relief.

Everything seemed more hopeful partly because of an improving relationship with the Arts Council. First, Grey Gowrie had replaced Lord Palumbo as Chairman of the Arts Council of England in April. (In a twist of small-world fate, Lord Gowrie – a regular face in the Royal Opera House audience – had been the Conservative Minister for the Arts when Mrs Thatcher had commissioned the Priestley Report back in 1983 to look into the financial affairs of both the Royal Shakespeare Company and the Royal Opera House.) Second, Anthony Everitt had resigned as Secretary General.

Free of the shackles imposed by the job, Everitt no longer disguised his feelings about one half of the Royal Opera House's operations. 'I have been to the ballet for the first time in six months,' he wrote in the *Guardian,* reviewing Anthony Dowell's restaging of Mikhail Baryshnikov's restaging of Gorsky's restaging of Petipa's original *Don Quixote.* 'It is not my favourite art form ... I usually let the soupy music, ridiculous plots and the general atmosphere of total irrelevance to real life wash over me.'

Don Quixote was the first production The Royal Ballet had presented at Covent Garden since returning from its American tour at the beginning of May. It was not remarkable that Anthony Everitt did not like it – the music by Minkus is rather workaday and the ballet itself little more than a series of virtuoso set pieces – few critics did. What was extraordinary was Everitt's attack on ballet audiences in general, as being driven in part by nostalgia and escapism and in part by lust: 'Both the rules of classical movement and the conventions of costume design,' he had expanded, 'draw explicit if idealized attention to their genital areas'.

It had to be better, then, for the Royal Opera House that Mary Allen – Anthony Everitt's Deputy and ex-actress, as the papers delighted in pointing out – had replaced him. The top job at the Arts Council was no longer in the hands of someone who doubted the value of much of what the House was trying to do. By the summer, the Gowrie/Allen accession had already heralded better relations between the two institutions.

Thursday, 30 June, was a red-letter day in the Westminster City Council chamber. The Royal Opera House finally heard formal planning permission granted for Phase II of the Development. Specific comments from English Heritage – one of the bodies whose consent had to be sought for the scheme – were still outstanding, but its support in general was assured. At last the Auditorium could be overhauled, The Royal Ballet could move to Covent Garden. The modern state-of-the-art backstage area might become a reality, after all these years. 'This is the final green light for us with the Development programme,' Keith Cooper said when interviewed by the press. 'The next stage is fund-raising.'

In the June heat, behind-the-scenes' optimism was tempered by the knowledge that

The third piece in the June Mixed Programme
was the world première of Ashley Page's *Fearful Symmetries*, also created with Irek Mukhamedov in mind.
In April 1995, the production team won an Olivier award for Best New Dance. In the dressing room
in June 1994, Page talks to Irek's partner, Ann De Vos.

OPPOSITE Principal
Character Artist David Drew makes up.

major skirmishes lay ahead. And, as national newspapers carried the announcement that
the House intended to approach the Millennium Fund for a third of the cost of the
Development scheme – maybe as much as £50 million – the Covent Garden Community
Association angrily voiced its outrage. 'The Royal Opera House is still ignoring all the criticism and requesting money from the National Lottery Fund to build an ugly opera house
which most people will never enter because they cannot afford the price of a ticket,' raged
Judy Monahan. 'We will continue to protest,' threatened her brother Jim, 'because the
scheme is bad for the area.'

'I'm known for my scruffiness. But it was a First Night,

so at least I was in a suit. I stood at the front

of the stage, prompt-side, just in view – and sang ...'

David Syrus, Head of Music for The Royal Opera

JULY & AUGUST

Sunday, 10 July, mid-morning, a makeshift stage in the Africa Centre, Covent Garden. BECTU official Gerry Morrissey and Chief Steward Peter Coggon sat at a trestle table. Some forty members of the stage crew were lined up in front of them on rows of chairs. They looked stroppy. The heatwave had continued and there were one or two reddened shoulders, a few angry lobster arms.

'The negotiating team,' announced Peter Coggon, 'recommended rejecting the current package.' He thought the union should offer management the opportunity of going to ACAS for conciliation on the issues still outstanding, namely Sunday working and touring. Technically everything else had been agreed, although the questions from the floor betrayed members' reluctance to accept the inevitable even at this late stage: the loss of the three-day week, their resentment towards multi-skilling, their displeasure about rostered shifts.

'What's our legal position if we don't settle with management?' asked one very hot-and-bothered-looking member. 'Can they force us to work new contracts?' queried another, clearly unwilling to give up the fight.

An open ballot was decided upon. The voting papers were collected in a blue plastic crate. There was confusion over the technicalities: did they have the authority to count the votes here and now? Was the meeting even quorate? They decided they did have the authority and they were quorate. Peter had received five proxy votes, all of them against accepting the offer. There was a spattering of rather half-hearted applause when the result was

On 25 July 1994, Director of Personnel
Mike Morris brought over one-hundred hours of negotiating meetings with BECTU to a close.
'I find the interplay of forces and the process, a fascinating thing to be involved in,' he said.

announced: three in favour, thirty-seven against. Gerry Morrissey would talk to Mike Morris first thing in the morning.

'Good old ACAS – been there many times,' smiled Mike Morris wryly when he heard. He was sanguine, unruffled by the news. 'A slow and frustrating business,' he added. 'Industrial relations are always like that, unfortunately.' He had hoped that the last-ditch efforts of both negotiating teams might have avoided this date on 21 July at ACAS headquarters on the Euston Road. But he was not really surprised. These situations are often more political than practical, more to do with strategy than genuine disagreement. As it happened, Morris had been ACAS's inaugural client, the union representative for ITN. He had won that day for his members, just as he had won days since for management.

To a degree Mike Morris's own future was on the line, too. He had already had a slightly sticky senior management meeting a few weeks earlier. Unwilling to let disagreements over conditions for touring hold up the entire package – especially since they did not directly affect conditions within the House itself – Mike had gone to explain the 'cost-neutral' arrangement he had worked out for the interim period. In the humid and scratchy meeting, possibly exacerbated by the fact that it was the opening night of *Aida*, he had found himself turned on by an impatient Opera Director Nicholas Payne and an irritable General Director Jeremy Isaacs. 'If this package fails, then they will wonder whether they were right in appointing me,' mused Mike. But he expected it to succeed and was confident that the new Stage Agreement would be in place by the beginning of next season. 'I find the interplay of forces and the process,' he admitted with a tongue-in-cheek smile, 'a fascinating thing to be involved in.'

Four days after the trip to ACAS, management issued a letter to the workforce. It outlined concessions in the areas in which they had been unable to reach agreement unaided: the running team was assured 150 hours of Sunday working for the 1994/95 and 1995/96 seasons; touring would now be contractual, but a premium would be paid on top of basic salary for those who did go; a limit of twenty-five hours per season was set for compulsory overnight working by members of the project teams. The finishing line was in sight.

BECTU unanimously accepted the offer. Four project teams of thirteen-apiece and a thirty-two-person running team would report for work at the beginning of September. After over a hundred hours of meetings, everything was at last settled.

For Mike Morris, though, these negotiations had barely scratched the surface. 'I'm a man in a hurry,' he warned. 'We're heading at breakneck speed towards 1997 when the House will close. Much will be demanded of our staff then ...'

The finishing line was in sight for the Opera Company, too – just three weeks to go. 'The idea is to end the Season with a big bang, this year *Aida*, surrounded by smaller shows,' said Opera Company Manager Terri-Jayne Gray. 'As we get further on in June and July though, we're literally on our knees. The orchestra's exhausted.'

Temperatures in the Pit continued to hit twenty-eight to twenty-nine degrees centigrade day in, night out, as The Royal Opera prepared for its last-but-one First Night of the Season. Massenet's *Manon* was only a 'smaller show' in the sense that it was a revival. Sir Colin Davis – Bernard Haitink's popular predecessor as Music Director – was to conduct and Romanian soprano Leontina Vaduva was returning to sing Manon, the role for which she

Ron Freeman, Wig and Make-Up Master, attempts to get Italian tenor Giuseppe Sabbatini ready to go on stage as the Chevalier Des Grieux in Massenet's *Manon*.

had won the 1988 Olivier Award for the Most Outstanding Achievement in Opera; and baritone Anthony Michaels-Moore, increasingly a House favourite, was to play her manipulative brother Lescaut.

Saturday, 2 July. All covers (understudies) had to ring in by lunchtime on the day of the performance, just in case there was a chance – however remote – that they might be needed. (Most spend their time sitting in the Royal Opera House canteen during performances, playing cards.) The singer covering Lescaut lived quite a way out of London and, since everything had seemed fine, he had been told not to bother dragging himself all the way into the centre of town.

But at six o'clock, an hour before the First-Night curtain was due up, Terri-Jayne Gray was trying to arm-twist a doctor into giving up his Saturday evening at very short notice. Anthony Michaels-Moore had started to run a temperature and felt rather sick. The doctor finally gave in – although he could not arrive until after seven. As Lescaut is a role that few baritones have in their repertoire, there was no one in the chorus who knew the part. Unwell, as he was, Anthony Michaels-Moore would simply have to muddle through.

For most of Act I he seemed to be coping – until, that is, he failed to reappear after one of his exits. On stage, Richard Van Allan, Philip Doghan and Eric Garrett imaginatively improvised a finale to the Act *without* Lescaut, watched by Colin Davis from the Pit and an alarmed David Syrus, Head of Music, from the Staff Box.

As soon as Act I had finished, David Syrus and Stuart Maunder – the in-House Director responsible for *Manon* – rushed backstage. 'I was in the Prompt corner holding the sick bag for Anthony,' said Terri-Jayne. As she and the doctor coped with the now very ill Anthony Michaels-Moore, Colin Davis phoned from the Pit to say that David Syrus would have to sing the role prompt-side of the stage, while Stuart Maunder walked the part on stage. Short of cancelling the remainder of the performance, it was the only option.

'I am less inhibited than other members of the Music Department,' Syrus admitted, 'and don't mind singing at public rehearsals. It's a bit of a joke – whenever I'm announced, the orchestra groans. But in a *proper* performance ...'

All non-essential stage entries were cut – mainly in Acts III and V – and the orchestra and cast were warned. Because it was a First Night, at least David was dressed in a suit – rather than his customary shorts and T-shirt – although he still had open-toed sandals on his

Nicola Martinucci (left) as Dick Johnson in Puccini's Western thriller *La fanciulla del West*. Gwyneth – the Voice – Jones sang saloon-bar hostess Minnie for the first time at Covent Garden as the Chorus sweltered in their coats and stetsons.

feet. Standing on the right-hand side of the Stage at the front, just in view so that his voice would carry, he sang while the semi-costumed Maunder mimed his way through the remainder of the opera: a kind of *Sprechgesang*, as the *Sunday Telegraph* put it. 'We both felt pretty shocked by it, really,' said Syrus afterwards. 'And the thought that some people had paid more than a hundred pounds for their tickets somewhat constricted my throat.'

'Karaoke At The Garden' headlined the *Evening Standard* the next day. It was left to Jeremy Isaacs — and Nicholas Payne — to deal with the letters of complaint ...

The Royal Ballet had been working its way through complicated, last-ditch arrangements, too. Between returning from America at the beginning of May — and going back there for a two-week Season at the New York Met in July — the Company had been working very hard: *Don Quixote, Fearful Symmetries, Winter Dreams, Danses concertantes.* (Sylvie Guillem's brilliance in *Quixote* had — allegedly — even led to *The Times* critic paying to see her a second time!)

Among others, both she and Darcey Bussell had also made guest appearances away from Covent Garden. In a Season where the fiery Sylvie had been in the news several times for refusing to dance what had been asked of her — the *Winter Gala* in December, the Crusaid Gala in March — the open-air Hampton Court Palace Festival wisely allowed her to assemble her own programme. She had chosen *Bolero* and *Sissi* — roles created for her by the choreographer Maurice Béjart — and her signature piece, *Herman Schmerman*, by William Forsythe. (Forsythe had been the first choreographer to fashion a role for the teenager already giving outstanding performances at the Paris Opéra Ballet.) She wanted Adam Cooper, as always, to partner her in *Herman Schmerman*. The problem was that he had already arranged to appear at Drury Lane with Darcey Bussell that same evening — Sunday 12 June — in a gala for London City Ballet.

Neither ballerina was inclined to give way. So, living up to his nickname, on that hot Sunday evening Super Cooper had danced with Darcey, then leapt into a taxi and charged westwards across London and out the other side. Two hours later, he was back in his yellow Versace skirt partnering Sylvie ...

A fortnight later, the whole Royal Ballet had gone West. Two weeks at the New York

Peter Abegglen
relaxing in one of the ballet dressing rooms.

Met was to be the crowning glory of its 1994 American tour. And so it had been, despite the absence of a disappointed Darcey Bussell who was resting an injured foot. Even the acerbic *New York Post* axe-man, Clive Barnes, had been impressed. '*Beauty* isn't a pretty picture' had been the spring headline for his review of the Company in Washington. In summertime New York, he was more positive: 'What started to be apparent three years ago now seems a certainty. Dowell, and his teaching team, have pulled the standards of dancing up by the bootstraps (or, more appropriately, toe-shoe ribbons), with The Royal Ballet dancing better now than at any time since the early 1970s.' Twelve weeks is clearly a long time in ballet ...

Now, at the beginning of August, The Royal Ballet was back in London for good: no more airports, no more coaches, no more Intercity trains.

The Opera Company and orchestra were on their last legs. They had bowed out with Puccini on Saturday, 23 July, finishing its Season as it had started. *La fanciulla del West,* with its virginal, Bible-reading, saloon-bar hostess Minnie – played somewhat implausibly by fifty-seven-year-old Welsh diva, Dame Gwyneth Jones – had perhaps not been the most obvious production with which to close the 1993/94 Season. But at last they had been released to their holidays. The Royal Ballet had another thirteen performances to go.

For thirty-seven-year-old Ashley Page – increasingly seen as The Royal Ballet's resident choreographer, albeit without the title – it had been a very busy Season. *Fearful Symmetries*, his jazzy and minimalist-scored ballet, had been prèmiered at Covent Garden earlier in the summer. It was an imaginative, bravado piece, that allowed Irek Mukhamedov's strength and power and seamless phrasing to dazzle audiences not hitherto aware that a human body could do so much. Now at the tail-end of the Season, Ashley Page's *Renard* was to have its first London showing. *Renard* had been premièred in the intimate spaces of the *Dance Bites* three-city mini-tour back in February. Successfully transferring the ballet to the generous Covent Garden stage would prove a challenge for the tired dancers.

Most of the critics who had been left in the London heat thought *Renard* equal to the challenge. 'What looked like a cartoon sketch in Cambridge,' wrote Judith Mackrell in the *Independent*, 'now has much darker more dangerous elements.'

'For the first time, I have felt like a full-time choreographer,' said Ashley Page. 'Next year I have absolutely nothing, but maybe it's a good idea considering that I'm just about to become a father.' His wife, Nicola Roberts – a First Soloist with the Company – was expecting their first baby any day.

As in life, art. For women working in most areas of the live performing arts, trying to combine pregnancy and motherhood with a demanding career is still a near-impossible juggling act. Terri-Jayne Gray, for example, is one of the most senior women in the Royal Opera House hierarchy. Her next logical move would be into some sort of Artistic Administrator post. 'But when I look at the women above me in the regional companies,' she said, 'they're all single and without kids. It is indicative of the hours we work. They are long and they are awkward.'

Pregnancy also makes additional physical demands on the already tiring lives of performers. For opera singers, the growing baby pushing up against the diaphragm means that it can be difficult to support the voice after about the seventh month of pregnancy. The problems are even more acute for dancers. Ballerinas are notorious for trying to take pregnancy in their stride, despite having long and painful labours. None the less, the daily punishment, inflicted by most dancers on their bodies is impossible to take when pregnant, most stopping many months before their babies are due.

Nicola Roberts had intended to work for as long as she was physically capable. But dancing in *Tales of Beatrix Potter* near the beginning of her pregnancy, both the demands of the role and the heavy mask made her feel too vulnerable. She called a halt and immediately felt relieved. Apart from her obsession with weight-gain – the habit of a lifetime being hard to break – her only other professional worry was losing her place in the Company scheme of things while she was away.

Ballet is an uncertain young person's profession and can be brutal for those for whom a new role within the Company cannot be found. Some, like Derek Rencher who joined the Company in 1953, become Character Artists, taking on roles that require acting and grace and style rather than alarming physical exploits. Princes mature into Kings. Even Anthony Dowell dances character roles – he opened as the spindle-waving Carabosse in the London Royal première of *The Sleeping Beauty* the following November – as does the Ballet Mistress of The Royal Ballet, Rosalind Eyre.

Classical choreography is still overwhelmingly a male pursuit and in any generation there are unlikely to be more than one or two dancers whose talent assures them a continuing place in this capacity within the Company. Both William Tuckett and Matthew Hart are being encouraged along this track, snapping at Page's heels. A couple of Principal ballerinas have risen up through the administrative or teaching hierarchy. Two outstanding dancers of Dowell's generation – Monica Mason and Dame Merle Park – achieved alternative success within The Royal Ballet (Mason as Assistant Director of The Royal Ballet and Dame Merle as Director of The Royal Ballet School), but most women find that age propels them into careers outside the Company. And rare is the Principal ballerina who is also a mother.

Nicola Roberts had three role models within the Company, though. Soloist Tracy Brown (whose husband Christopher Saunders is also a Soloist with the Company), Principal Fiona Chadwick and Lesley Collier had returned: Tracy's son Peter was now fourteen months old, Fiona's daughter Emily nearly three and Lesley's twin sons slightly older.

A member of the Company since 1978, Fiona had been promoted to Principal back in 1984, a couple of years before Anthony Dowell took over from Norman Morrice as Director of The Royal Ballet. Despite broken nights and rushing around like any working parent to spend as much time as possible with her daughter, Chadwick even felt that motherhood had improved her skill. 'Having a baby gave my dancing a new lease of life,' she said. 'I felt much more confident and I seemed to have so much stamina, I felt like superwoman.' Her amazing return to Class just five weeks after her emergency Caesarian had gone down in Company folklore ...

Like Ashley Page, Fiona Chadwick had had a good year. In January she had had excellent notices for her portrayal of Countess Larisch in *Mayerling*. And when she had danced in the world première of *The Sleeping Beauty* in Washington in April, almost every newspaper on both sides of the Atlantic had run her impromptu banter with President Clinton about him needing his own Lilac Fairy. Then, at another performance of *Beauty*, this time in Texas, she had started the performance as a Lilac Fairy and finished it as a Princess, swapping tutus midstream when Lesley Collier, dancing Aurora, had torn her calf-muscle on stage. Chadwick had almost never been injured in her career and this was her enduring reputation within the Company, a real trooper who was never too grand to help out.

On Saturday, 6 August, the closing day of the 1993/94 Ballet Season, she was one of the two Juliets due to dance in *Romeo and Juliet*. During the year, Prokofiev's Verona had seen ten Juliets in three different productions in London alone – including Bussell, Guillem and Durante as well as an acclaimed début from young First Artist, Sarah Wildor. There had been criticism about the punters lack of choice, but audiences were still coming to the Royal Opera House. The August crowd was usually boosted by one or two enterprising tourists along with the die-hard aficionados and children on summer-holiday treats. Fiona Chadwick and Adam Cooper were to dance the matinée, followed by Viviana Durante and Irek Mukhamedov at seven o'clock.

Between performances, though, there was a tradition to be honoured. Dame Ninette de

Terry Keen with scimitar in the Armoury at the very top of the Royal Opera House building. The muskets, rifles and daggers are all historically authentic.

Valois – founder of The Royal Ballet and The Birmingham Royal Ballet – had introduced the ceremony of the taglioni cake as the final goodbye to each Season. By tradition, the seed cake was cut with Iago's dagger from Verdi's opera *Otello* – borrowed from Terry Keen in the Armoury – and shared by everyone who had contributed to the work of the Company over the year.

Now, with the ceremony about to start, the Ballet Rest Area at the Royal Opera House

Last Rites. The Royal Ballet hung up its shoes on Saturday, 6 August. Fiona Chadwick (above) danced Juliet at the matinée of Prokofiev's *Romeo and Juliet*, having been told that after sixteen years with the Company – ten of those as Principal – her services were no longer required. An audience of friends, fans and family gave her one of the longest curtain calls of the Season. A few hours later it was the turn of fêted Italian star Viviana Durante (opposite) to accept the floral tributes.

was squashed. Fiona Chadwick among others was missing, but most of the dancers had found themselves a spot. Administrators, management, répétiteurs and music staff had squeezed in, too, as had Joan McKenzie who had made the cake for thirty-six of its thirty-seven-year history. It was a boiling hot August day, bare-arms weather. Limbs covered every inch of the floor, legs stuck straight out in front, pointed feet flopped sideways at ease. A few dancers hung over the bannisters, watching those who were leaving the Company called up by Anthony Dowell to accept small mementoes of their time with The Royal Ballet. Some looked more embarrassed at this than others: Neil Geraghty was going to train as a physiotherapist; the Assistant Ballet Mistress Jacqui Tallis was moving on after twenty-four years with the Company; Matthew Trent was joining The Australian Ballet; and Principal Character Artist Stephen Wicks had decided to open his own flower shop in Covent Garden.

On Saturday, 6 August, at nearly two o'clock, the Percussion section was in the Pit checking that the array of bells, triangles, blocks and drums needed for *Romeo and Juliet* were ready. Backstage, Act I Beginners had been called and the Wings were full of Capulets, Montagues and their knives. One or two administrators were also backstage. There was an unusual atmosphere: an overwhelming tension suspended in the still air, heightened emotion. Michael Waldman and his BBC crew were alert.

Juliet herself is not on stage until Scene Two. Fiona Chadwick had danced the role many, many times, and it was her photograph that the House had used in its programme. 'I've been asked to leave, unfortunately,' she told Michael Waldman and his crew in a voice that gave nothing away. In the matinée audience were her family, her friends and the fans she had built up during her sixteen years with The Royal Ballet.

Feeling within the Company was running very high. Dancers were stunned. 'She's been shafted,' spat out a male First Artist, 'and no one knows why.' There was a great deal of mutinous gossip, speculation, insecurity. If it could happen to Fiona, after all she had done for the Company, then no one was safe. 'I heard *they* think she's lost her figure,' said a young woman in the Corps. 'Her face doesn't fit,' suggested another. Loyal to the last, Fiona Chadwick was being discreet about the decision – not least because under the terms of her contract she was entitled to work a full Season's notice.

Fiona took one of the longest curtain calls of the entire Season, fifteen minutes of applause, flowers of all colours showering down on to the Stage. Someone even threw a bouquet. Adam Cooper picked it up and presented it to her with great panache. She accepted the tributes with elegance, professional to the last.

When Irek Mukhamedov and Viviana Durante danced the roles a few hours later, finishing off the Season, it was not really surprising that there was almost a sense of anti-climax in the Wings …

'Nobody among us knows what is going to happen here
come 1997 when we have to close.
There is only one person who knows,
and that's Jeremy Isaacs.'

George New, Scenic Artist

F I N A L E

Jeremy Isaacs actually did not yet know what would happen in 1997, either to the building or the thousand and more people who worked in it. Another Season had passed and now there were only three more years before the Royal Opera House had to shut down. If anything, the closure and the redevelopment programme – not to mention the money needed to finance it – would cast an even darker shadow during the 1994/95 Season than it had during the preceding eleven months or so. Although not yet public knowledge, Jeremy Isaacs himself had agreed with the Board to step down in summer 1997, 'when I shall be sixty-five and shall have even longer grey hair than I do now.' It was not unlikely that Bernard Haitink would choose to go then too, leaving the way clear for a new team to take possession of, what Isaacs called, 'the promised land of a redeveloped Royal Opera House'.

'I should imagine some of us will be leaving come the close down,' Jean Flower, Cleaning Supervisor, admitted. Jean has worked at the House for thirteen years. 'I don't know what's going to happen when they do eventually reopen, whether they will have contract cleaners in. We'll just have to wait and see what happens.' Her concern for the future was shared by most and at the last full staff meeting of the Season very little else was discussed. Jeremy Isaacs got to his feet in the Auditorium, wedged between two rows in the Orchestra Stalls, his back to the crimsoned-curtained Stage. As always, Margaret Stevenson – Flipper – stood at his elbow. A member of the twenty-eight-strong cleaning team, she is by tradition the first to ask a question of the General Director at House meetings. Isaacs told the hot Auditorium that the general idea was to return to Covent Garden in July 1999, then gradually build up to a full performing programme by December of that year. So far as job security was concerned – from 1997 itself to taking possession of the newly-refurbished theatre two years later – until a decision had been made about what would happen to The Royal Opera and The Royal Ballet companies during the closure period it would be impossible to give specific assurances. To anybody.

There were three options: relocation to another London theatre; one or both of the companies working on a project basis; and total closure. Total closure – either by maintaining a skeleton performing and workshop staff with rehearsal facilities or by laying off over ninety per cent of employees – would cost a fortune by the time redundancy payments had been taken into account. The public would see nothing for the £30 million or so spent on its behalf and what's more, the artistic cost would be incalculable: two world-class opera and ballet companies – not to mention orchestra and skilled workshop staff – which had been built up over generations would be sacrificed overnight. No one really considered closure a feasible option, whatever the Joint Action Committee at the Arts Council - since 1 April known as the Arts Council of England - might have threatened back in February.

The House had rejected the idea of splitting the companies from one another and operating them on a project basis – an opera gig here, a dance gig there. As with closure, there was the same argument against scattering clarinetists, milliners, ballerinas, répétiteurs to the four winds. There were already highly-successful ballet and opera companies, committed to national touring, from their own Birmingham Royal Ballet to the Welsh National Opera and English National Ballet. And the costs of taking the Royal Opera House on tour had been estimated at about £300 000 pounds per week – hardly an inexpensive way forward.

No, there was only one option: the House had to find itself a home-from-home for the closure period and relocate *in toto*. The difficulty was that there were few theatres in London which could cope with the huge demands of opera and, to a lesser degree, ballet.

The theatre needing the least renovation to make it technically suitable was the Theatre Royal in Drury Lane, just round the corner from the House's present location in Bow Street. Throughout the 1993/94 Season the Theatre Royal had been cited as a possible billet for The Royal Opera and The Royal Ballet during closure, despite categoric denials from its owners Cameron Mackintosh that the highly-successful musical *Miss Saigon* would be moved to make way for the invaders from round the corner. (The *Miss Saigon* team held its own on the cricket field, too, dismissing the Royal Opera House's team for just twenty-nine runs.) By the late summer Cameron Mackintosh's message got through and the House had to accept that the Theatre Royal's owners would not change their mind.

The gentlemen and ladies of the Main Board:
(clockwise from left) Bamber Gascoigne, Sir John Manduell, Sir Kit McMahon, Chris Lowe,
Baroness Blackstone, Lady MacMillan, Andrew Tuckey, Mrs Vivien Duffield,
Bob Gavron, Jim Butler and Keith Cooper. (Jeremy Isaacs, Sir Angus Stirling,
Sir James Spooner, Clive Timms and Mike Morris are out of shot.) In the street outside,
the mercury was nudging thirty degrees.

A few hundred yards away at the bottom of Bow Street is the derelict Lyceum Theatre. Used as a dance hall during the Second World War (as was the Royal Opera House), the Lyceum had not staged a performance for over twenty years and now stood abandoned to pigeons and drunks and fast-food wrappings. But at the beginning of July, the Theatres Trust announced that it had given its blessing to a £15 million restoration scheme by Apollo Leisure, who was happy to consider the House as a temporary tenant. There were draw-backs, though. The Lyceum had several technical limitations, so would need substantial addi-tional sums of money spent on it to make it a suitable home-from-home for the House. It would also be ready in 1996, which left the possible spectre of the House paying a holding rent on a theatre that it was not actually going to need for another nine months or so.

Sadler's Wells in north London – due to be refurbished between the beginning of 1996 and the autumn of 1997 – was the third possibility. Rental would be considerably lower than

This mural dominates the corner
of Russell Street and the Covent Garden piazza, a colourful indication
of just how strong is some local opposition
to the Royal Opera House's redevelopment plans.

Everything from tiaras to trilbies
is 'magicked' out of the cramped warren of the millinery department.

most West End sites, but its capacity was only seventy-five per cent of the House's and, as top prices were lower than at Covent Garden, there would be a significant loss of income.

During the Season, the Board had commissioned several reports. The cumulative result was an attraction for the idea of building a temporary permanent base for the House's operations during its two years in exile from Covent Garden. It would need about eight acres, so obviously this would have to be a less central site. In a park perhaps? Battersea? Vauxhall? But, at least, the House would have the advantage of a new home being tailor-made to its requirements. It would also be easier for the House to sustain its existing public image and *modus operandi* intact. And, since the Royal Opera House would be returning home in 1999, the tailor-made structure could then be handed over for Millennial Festivals and the like. 'The Royal Parks are only considered in pencil, as it were,' admitted Keith Cooper, 'but we have commissioned a feasibility study and are making tentative overtures!'

The decision about relocation was, of course, partly dependent on money. The House would have to close in 1997, come what may. Twenty million pounds was the price-tag put on maintaining operations during the closure period, money that would have to be found from somewhere. The essential restoration work required by European Union Health and Safety directives would take about nineteen months and cost something in the region of £25 million (not to mention the additional £10 million needed to bring the administration offices in Floral Street up to scratch). There would be nothing new to show for this expenditure, just a patched up nineteenth-century Royal Opera House.

The actual price of developing the site as a twenty-first century opera house to rival the best in the world was now estimated at £193.8 million: forty per cent of this would come from the realization of property assets; thirty per cent from a Public Appeal, led by Mrs Vivien Duffield and Lord Sainsbury and masterminded by Keith Cooper (soon-to-be announced as the inaugural Director of Corporate Affairs); and the final thirty per cent – £58.5 million – would come from the Lottery. They hoped.

In the last Main Board meeting of the Season at the end of July, the discussion was of little else. The occasional aside about applications to the Lottery being a lottery escaped from one or two lips in the lethargic summer heat. A National Lottery operator – Camelot – was

'In two years time,
I can turn round and say I've done forty years in the business,
man and boy. And I don't think there's any single painter in London
at this moment who can actually say that.' Even though the audiences are on holiday,
the behind-the-scenes work goes on. George New (above) mixes, while at the paintframe
Malcolm Key (opposite) sketches the initial image on to the eighteen metres (sixty foot)
backcloth with a long-handled charcoal stick.

now firmly in place and intending to start selling tickets in November 1994. The initial
deadline for submissions to all five Lottery Funds – the arts, sport, national heritage, charitable projects and initiatives to mark the year 2000 – was to be January 1995. Between now
and then, the Board wanted sympathetic journalists to cover the House's case so that the
drip, drip, drip media diet of unwarranted subsidy and inflated ticket prices would not preju-
dice those who would be giving out the cash. Jeremy Isaacs felt that publicity for their hundreds of less glamorous, lower-profile projects – particularly the work of their dynamic
Education Department – was the key to wider-spread public support. 'We should let them
know,' he emphasized, 'that we have even subjected ourselves to the agonies and miseries of
a BBC television crew shooting up our nostrils for four days out of every working six in

order to put across to the public the message that it is hard work putting stuff on the stage and that we deserve a bit of support.'

Everyone was hot and everyone was tired. There was still confusion as to whether they should approach the Millennium Commission, the Arts Council or even the National Heritage Fund. If the Commission, then perhaps each of the nine Commissioners should be invited to lunch by a member of the Board? 'I'd be surprised if they would be prepared to come to an individual bribing session,' commented Bamber Gascoigne.

In the end – with a document nearly an inch thick – the House applied to the Arts Council's National Lottery Board for £58.5 million (a third of the cost of the Development), plus the £20 million transitional costs for the closure period itself. Certain parts of the project – listed buildings such as the Floral Hall – might be eligible for Heritage Fund money. And, if the Royal Opera House did build a temporary home from scratch, a theatre that would become available for turn-of-the-century festivals and celebrations, the House might approach the Millennium Commission for financing for that.

It was a long meeting: until they knew how much – if any – money they would have from the Lottery, it was impossible to make decisions and they would not know that for nearly another year from now when the closure had inched even closer. Chicken-and-egg.

August is the quietest month in the Royal Opera House: no performances, empty chairs in the administrative and managerial offices. But work still goes on in the workshops: milliners, seamstresses, set-builders, scenic artists, poster designers. Everything has to be ready for the First Night of the new Season, summer holidays or not.

In the paintframe – an immense expanse where painters create the backcloths that fill the stage – the scenic artists were working on beautiful colours and designs that would dazzle next year's audiences. George New has worked at the Royal Opera House for twenty-five years. 'In two years time I can turn round and say I've done forty years in this business, man and boy.' The team of artists copy the image from a sketch, then work with the designer until the proportions and shades and shapes are right. The dimensions are mind-boggling – eighteen metres by eleven metres (sixty feet by thirty-five feet). Sometimes they work on canvas, other times on more expensive materials such as sheeting, even though the way a ballet or opera is lit can make a mockery of the time and expertise spent at the paintframe. 'We're allowed to see the Dress Rehearsal,' explained George, 'and we look at the scenery and hanging cloths and sometimes say that wasn't worth doing because it's all in darkness!' Despite his years of service in the House, he seemed sanguine about his future come 1997. 'Safe? My job is no more safe than anyone else's. I'd miss working here, but I would manage. I've got so many other hobbies and things. But it's nice to have music every morning when you come in. Some of it you don't like, but you get used to it. My wife was a great Wagner fan and she introduced me to Wagner. And I thought it was the greatest thing I ever heard. I still do.'

Away from the paintframe, others were at work, too. Just as last year, the 1994/95 Season was due to start with Puccini followed by Rossini followed by Wagner. The first new productions – *Das Rheingold* and *Die Walküre* – would be premièred on consecutive nights in October. Music Director Bernard Haitink would conduct, with *Siegfried* – the third part of Wagner's *Der Ring des Nibelungen* – to follow in the spring. Royal Opera Director Nicholas Payne had commissioned the dynamic Richard Jones/Nigel Lowery partnership to come up with a cut-price *Ring*, the only full cycle of the opera planned in Britain for the end of the twentieth century. Jones and Lowery were notorious on the European opera circuit for their unorthodox, some say visionary, productions. As a consequence, Nicholas Payne had spent much of the 1993/94 Season trying to reassure his Music Director Bernard Haitink that the director/designer team would *not* sacrifice musical values to gimmickry. 'They have devised a *Ring* unencumbered by tradition,' Payne hammered out with commitment. 'They have drawn on a kaleidoscope of references and images, yet fashioned something which is both original and truly theirs.'

When the designs arrived – late – Bernard Haitink was passionately unconvinced by Richard Jones's and Nigel Lowery's interpretation which included stretch limousines, lollipop men and Rhine-maidens who looked less like creatures of Norse myth than like Michelin women on a garage forecourt. The set itself was a gigantic wooden whale's mouth. 'Do you think the audience will understand that?' he challenged Nicholas Payne in a difficult meeting over plans to squeeze in a jet aeroplane. 'We should not be too arrogant and should not take too much for granted. I may be old-fashioned, God knows, but ...' Nicholas Payne, however, persevered and, by August 1994, a cast of celebrated Wagnerians, John Tomlinson and Jane Henschel among them, were already stuck into eight weeks of rehearsal with Director Richard Jones. The artists love working with him,' said Keith Cooper, 'they feel supported and inspired. That surely should count for something.'

The summer holidays were over. Jeremy Isaacs, General Director of the Royal Opera House, sat in his office. A car alarm pierced the quiet of the street below. He smoothed down one of his elegant, eye-grabbing silk ties. In just over a week the 1994/95 Season would kick off, opera followed seven weeks later by the ballet. And, by the time the House closed its doors for its summer break eleven months later, hundreds of thousands of people would have been dazzled by Mozart and Britten, Rossini and Wagner and Tchaikovsky – something for everyone.

There was a glittering line-up of performers expected: Luciano Pavarotti, Bryn Terfel, Georg Solti, Charles Mackerras, Anne Sofie von Otter, Angela Gheorghiu, Amanda Roocroft. Guillem, Bussell, Durante and friends would be dancing in specially commissioned ballets, including pieces by dance bad-boy Michael Clark and the inspirational William Forsythe. And the British première of *The Sleeping Beauty.* There was a sparkling line-up of opera productions too: Puccini's *Turandot* – home of the most popular aria of all time, *Nessun Dorma* – would open the Season on 12 September. On its heels were *Das Rheingold* and *Die Walküre.* And Richard Eyre's opera début with *La traviata.* And Jonathan Miller's *Così fan tutte,* as costumed by Armani. The Royal Opera House, surely, was a British cultural institution of which to be proud. And yet the mantra – redevelopment, ticket prices, Lottery, value-for-money, subsidy, élitist, closure, restoration – droned on.

On Monday, 12 September 1994, at eight a.m., Peter Meade, Head Stage Door Keeper, opened the grille and took in the milk. One hundred pints.

LIST OF 1993/94 PRODUCTIONS AT
THE ROYAL OPERA HOUSE AND ON TOUR

*The year of the première of an opera or ballet is
given in brackets after its title.*

THE ROYAL OPERA

Season opened 11 September 1993 and
closed 23 July 1994

Madama Butterfly – Giacomo Puccini (1904)
11 September 1993
Revival conducted by Carlo Rizzi

L'Italiana in Algeri –
Gioachino Rossini (1813)
18 September 1993
Revival conducted by Carlo Rizzi
(The Cluff Foundation)

Die Meistersinger von Nürnberg –
Richard Wagner (1869)
8 October 1993
New production conducted by Bernard
Haitink and directed by Graham Vick
(Cable & Wireless plc and The Friends of
Covent Garden)

Mitridate, rè di Ponto –
Wolfgang Amadeus Mozart (1770)
15 October 1993
Revival conducted by Paul Daniel
(The Friends of Covent Garden)

Eugene Onegin –
Peter Ilyich Tchaikovsky (1879)
21 October 1993
Revival conducted by Mark Ermler
(The Drogheda Circle)

Die Zauberflöte – Mozart (1791)
15 November 1993
New production conducted by Andrew
Parrott and David Syrus (Performances
supported by Dr Stanley Ho OBE, C St J)

Tosca – Puccini (1900)
4 December 1993
Revival conducted by Edward Downes

Carmen – Georges Bizet (1875)
21 January 1994/19 April 1994

Revival conducted by Jeffrey Tate
and Jacques Delacôte
(Daiwa Europe Limited and The Linbury Trust)

Elektra – Richard Strauss (1910)
26 January 1994
Revival conducted by Christian Thielemann

Chérubin – Jules Massenet (1905)
14 February 1994
New production conducted by
Mario Bernardi and Alistair Dawes and
directed by Tim Albery (KPMG and
The Jean Sainsbury Royal Opera House Fund)

Rigoletto – Giuseppe Verdi (1851)
19 February 1994
Revival conducted by Simone Young
and Paul Wynne Griffiths
(National Westminster Bank)

Katya Kabanova – Leoš Janáček (1921)
4 March 1994
New production conducted by
Bernard Haitink and directed by
Trevor Nunn (The Friends of Covent Garden
and the Royal Opera House Trust)

Un ballo in maschera – Verdi (1859)
12 March 1994
Revival conducted by Daniele Gatti
and Martin André

Gawain – Harrison Birtwistle (1991)
14 April 1994
Revival conducted by Elgar Howarth
(The John S Cohen Foundation and The Friends of
Covent Garden)

Le Nozze di Figaro – Mozart (1786)
25 April 1994
Revival conducted by Hartmut Haenchen
and Maurits Sillem (Citibank)

Fedora – Umberto Giordano (1898)
9 May 1994
New production conducted by Edward
Downes and directed by Lamberto Puggelli
(Union Bank of Switzerland)

Mosè in Egitto – Rossini (1818)
23 May 1994
New production conducted by Paolo Olmi
and directed by Hugo De Ana
(Peter Moores Foundation)

Aida – Verdi (1871)
16 June 1994
New production conducted by
Edward Downes and directed by
Elijah Moshinsky (The Peninsular and Oriental
Steam Navigation Company)

Manon – Massenet (1884)
2 July 1994
Revival conducted by Colin Davis
(Sir Philip and Lady Harris)

La fanciulla del West – Puccini (1910)
11 July 1994
Revival conducted by Richard Buckley
(Performances supported by Dr Stanley Ho
OBE, C St J)

THE ROYAL BALLET

Season opened 23 October 1993 and closed
6 August 1994

MIXED PROGRAMME –
WHITE HOT AND DIFFERENT
23 October 1993
Fanfare
Choreography by Matthew Hart (1993) and
music by Brian Elias
(The Friends of Covent Garden)
If This is Still a Problem
Choreography by William Tuckett (1993)
and music by Maurice Ravel
(The Friends of Covent Garden)
Herman Schmerman
Choreography by William Forsythe (Royal
Ballet première 1993) and music by
Thom Willems (The Friends of Covent Garden)
Different Drummer
Choreography by Kenneth MacMillan
(1984) and music by Anton Webern
and Arnold Schoenberg (Citibank)

Romeo and Juliet
29 October 1993/6 January 1994/
4 August 1994
Choreography by MacMillan (1965)
and music by Sergei Prokoviev (1938)
(Guinness Peat Group)

MIXED PROGRAMME
20 November 1993
Ballet Imperial
Choreography by George Balanchine
(Royal Ballet première 1950) and music
by Peter Ilyich Tchaikovsky
(The Friends of Covent Garden)
Tales of Beatrix Potter
Choreography by Frederick Ashton (1971),
staging by Anthony Dowell (1992)
and music by John Lanchbery
(The Jean Sainsbury Royal Opera House Fund and
The Friends of Covent Garden)

The Nutcracker
17 December 1993
Choreography by Peter Wright (1984)
and music by Tchaikovsky (1892)
(The British Printing and Communication
Corporation plc and Heron International plc)

Mayerling
28 January 1994
Choreography by MacMillan (1978)
and music by Franz Liszt (arranged
and orchestrated by Lanchbery)
(IBM United Kingdom Limited and
The Friends of Covent Garden)

DANCE BITES MINI-TOUR
(Tour sponsored by The Audrey Sacher Charitable
Trust and The Friends of Covent Garden)
7–15 February 1994 (Leicester,
Cambridge, Blackpool)
Desirable Hostilities
Choreography by Tuckett (1994)
and music by J S Bach
Monotones II
Choreography by Ashton (1965)
and music by Erik Satie
Caught Dance
Choreography by Hart (1994)
and music by Witold Lutoslawski (1959)
Renard
Choreography by Ashley Page (1994)
and music by Igor Stravinsky (1916)

MIXED PROGRAMME –
THE IMMORTAL HOURS
23 March 1994
The Dream
Choreography by Ashton (1964)
and music by Felix Mendelssohn (1843)
Tombeaux
Choreography by David Bintley (1993)
and music by William Walton (1963)
(The Friends of Covent Garden with a legacy
from Mrs Patricia M Wright)
A Month in the Country
Choreography by Ashton (1976)
and music by Frederick Chopin
(arranged by Lanchbery) (The Linbury Trust)

USA TOUR
6 April – 8 May 1994 (Washington,
West Palm Beach, Austin, Houston
and Orange County); 3–17 July 1994
(New York)
The Judas Tree
Choreography by MacMillan (1992)
and music by Brian Elias
The Sleeping Beauty
Choreography by Marius Petipa,
staging by Dowell (1994)
and music by Tchaikovsky (1890)
(Inchcape plc and The Friends of Covent Garden)
Mayerling (The Friends of Covent Garden)
Tales of Beatrix Potter
(The Jean Sainsbury Royal Opera House Fund
and The Friends of Covent Garden)
The Dream
A Month in the Country (The Linbury Trust)
Tombeaux (The Friends of Covent Garden
with a legacy from Mrs Patricia M Wright)
Herman Schmerman
(The Friends of Covent Garden)

Don Quixote
30 May 1994
Choreography by Mikhail Baryshnikov
(1978), staging by Dowell (1993)
and music by Ludwig Minkus (1869)
(arranged and orchestrated by
Christopher Palmer)
(The Linbury Trust
and The Friends of Covent Garden)

MIXED PROGRAMME
18 June 1994
Danses concertantes
Choreography by MacMillan (1955)
and music by Stravinsky (1942)

Winter Dreams
Choreography by MacMillan (1991) and
music by Tchaikovsky (arranged by Philip
Gammon) (The Friends of Covent Garden)
Fearful Symmetries
Choreography by Ashley Page (1994)
and music by John Adams (1988)

MIXED PROGRAMME
1 August 1994
A Month in the Country (The Linbury Trust)
Tombeaux (The Friends of Covent Garden with
a legacy from Mrs Patricia M Wright)
Renard (The Audrey Sacher Charitable Trust)

THE BIRMINGHAM ROYAL BALLET
Sylvia
28 March 1994
Choreography and staging by David Bintley
(1993) and music by Léo Delibes (1876)
(PowerGen plc)

MIXED PROGRAMME –
FROM STARS AND STRIPES
31 March 1994
Serenade
Choreography by Balanchine (1934)
and music by Tchaikovsky (1881)
Fall River Legend
Choreography by Agnes de Mille (1948)
and music by Morton Gould
(The Friends of Covent Garden)
Elite Syncopations
Choreography by MacMillan and others
and music by Scott Joplin (1904)

THE ROYAL OPERA HOUSE
Galas, Festivals and Guests 1993/94 Season

Don Quixote Gala
(Barclays Bank PLC, Hasbro UK Ltd.,
and Loewe Perfumes)

Winter Gala
1 December 1993

Gloriana – Benjamin Britten (1953)
7 February 1994
Opera North
(Nottinghamshire County Council with the help
of a substantial contribution from The Britten
Estate Limited)

The Royal Ballet School Matinée
16 July 1994

INDEX

Page numbers in *italic* refer to the illustrations

Abegglen, Peter 113, 119, 122, 127, *169*
ACAS 149, 162-3
Africa Centre 162
Agache, Alexandru 153
Aida 9, *140-1*, 150-3, *152*
Albery, Tim 95
Allen, Mary 71, 91, 159
Allen, Thomas 21
 Covent Garden Festival 147
 Die Meistersinger 33, 34
 Don Giovanni 9, 50
 Le nozze di Figaro 139
American tour 49, 86, 119, 142, 170
 BECTU 117
 police 127
 Tales of Beatrix Potter 122
Amphitheatre 16, 88
Anderson, Helen 102
Apollo Leisure 179
Arnold, Ivell 17-18, *18*, 153-4
Arts Council 11-12, 70, 92-3
 Chairman *see* Gowrie, Lord; Palumbo, Lord
 closure 178
 development funding 157
 headquarters 91
 National Lottery 184
 Phase II 159
 Secretary General *see* Allen, Mary; Everitt, Anthony
 Deputy *see* Allen, Mary
 subsidies 9, 66
 Warnock Report 26, 46
Arts Council of GB *see* Arts Council
Ashton, Frederick 19, 43, 74
atmosphere, opera & ballet companies 21
Auden, W.H. 7
audience, first-timers 80
Auditorium *10*, 12, *15*, 22, 24, *25*
 overhaul 11, 159
 Winter Gala 63-4
Australian Ballet 176

Balanchine, George 42, 71
ballet, nature of 21, 76
Ballet Imperial 20, 42, 71, 87
Un ballo in maschera 106, 153

Bamber, Larissa 127
Baron's Court 20, 22-3, 38
Barry, E.M. 10, 38
Baryshnikov, Mikhail 106
Bastille, Paris 11
BBC
 BBC2 63-4
 Double Exposure film crew 14, 26, 54, 56, 122
 Newsnight 138
 French & Saunders show 127
 outside broadcast (OB) 102
 Radio 3, 41, 102, 146
 television 46
Beckett, Samuel 51
Beckley, Christine 24, 26, *72-3*, *74-6*
BECTU 26, 30-1, 65-6, 149
 agreement 131
 American tour 117
 first meeting 142-3
 new contracts 162, 164
 reconstruction plans 65-6
Beecham, Sir Thomas 12
Beesley, Mark *140-1*
Béjart, Maurice 168
Benjamin, George 138
Benjamin, Leanne 39, 87, *89*
Bernardi, Mario *94*, 95, 97
Bernhardt, Sarah 146
Berra, Micky 122, 126, 130
Bevin, Ernie 47
Birmingham Royal Ballet 17, 38, 178
 Director *see* Wright, Sir Peter founder 175
Birtwistle, Sir Harrison 131, 134, 138
Bizet, Georges 77
Bjørnson, Maria 47, 49-50, 54
 Katya Kabanova 54, 117
 The Phantom of the Opera 105
 The Sleeping Beauty 47, 49-50, 113, *116*, 117, 130
Black, Jeffrey 138-9
Blackstone, Baroness Tessa 49-50, 130, *179*
BOC sponsorship 147
Bolshoi Ballet 20
Box Office 20, 56, 78
 jammed 71, 74, 148
 overhaul 112
Britten, Benjamin 32, 39, 186
Brown, Tracy 119, 172

Browne, Richard 23
Brueghel, Pieter 34
Bussell, Darcey 8, 40, 87, *107*, *107*, 170, 186
 guest appearances 168
 Nureyev Gala 108
 Romeo and Juliet 36, 172
 The Sleeping Beauty 110-11, *116*, *124-5*, 126-7, 130
 The Nutcracker 20
 Winter Gala 46
Butler, Jim 43, *179*

Callas, Maria 11-12
Camelot 182-3
Cameron, Mackintosh 178
Cardiff Bay Opera House Trust 92
Carmen 77-8, 80, 82, *84-5*
Carr, Christopher 42, 126
Carreras, José 8, *144*, 146-8
Caruso, Enrico 147
Cassidy, Michael 20-1
Caught Dance 104
Chadwick, Fiona 119
 Mayerling 90, 172
 Romeo and Juliet 172, *175*, 176
 The Nutcracker 20
 The Sleeping Beauty 130, 172
Character Artists 171
Chérubin 93, *94*, 95, *96*, *98-9*, *101*, 102, 104, 112
 First Night 100
children, dressing rooms 76
choreography 38, 160, 168, 171
Citibank 42
Clark, Felicity 43, 47, *67*
Clark, Michael 186
Clinton, President Bill 123, 130, 172
Coggon, Peter *27*, 31, 65, 143-4, 149, 162
Collier, Lesley 74, 172
comédie-chantée 93
Concertgebouw, Amsterdam 32
contemporary works 19
Cooper, Adam 87-8, 122, *156*
 Herman Schmerman 104, 168
 London City Ballet Gala 168
 Mayerling 90
 Romeo and Juliet 176
Cooper, Keith 39, 46, 91, 92, 105, 108, *109*, 131, *179*

absence 155
alternate site 180
Box Office 71, 74
Chérubin 102
Covent Garden Festival 148
Development programme 159
Public Appeal 182
reputation 112
Rozhdestvensky 97
Winter Gala 47
Cope, Jonathan 87
Corbett, Cliff 80, *94*
Così fan tutte 57, 186
Covent Garden
 audiences 39
 backstage 26, 74
 Friends 42-3, 46, 146-7
 chairman *see* Gascoigne, Bamber
 Phase II 12, 57, 155, 157
 Stage 23-24
 support 42
 theatre 15, 57
Covent Garden Community Association 160
 Chairman *see* Monahan, Jim
Covent Garden Festival 147-8
Covent Garden Opera Company 77
covers 166
Crisp, Clement 41
Crush Bar 16-17, *18*, 63, 138, 148, 155

Daily Mail 39
Daily Telegraph 97
Damonte, Magali 83, 86
Dance of the Apprentices 34-5
Dance Bites tour 86, 103, 170
Daniel, Paul 56
Danses concertantes 18, *156*, 168
Davis, Sir Colin 32, 134, 164, 166
Delacôte, Jacques 148
Desirable Hostilities 104
Díaz, Justino 153
Different Drummer 39
Dixon, Jeremy 59, 157
documentary films 14, 63, 88, 122
Doghan, Philip 166
Domingo, Plácido 46, *60*, 64, 78, 146
 Carmen 148

(Domingo, Plácido cont.)
  extra performance 148
  return 8
Don Giovanni 9, 50
Don Quixote 159, 168
double bills 20, 71
Dowell, Anthony 19, 39, 87,
  171
  Don Quixote 159
  If This Is Still A Problem 38,
    41
  Mayerling 90
  Royal Ballet School 24, 26,
    75
  The Sleeping Beauty 113, 117,
    127, *128-9*, 130
  teaching team 170
Downes, Sir Edward 32, 146,
  154
Drew, David *161*
Drogheda Circle 42-3
Duchess of Kent 46
Duffield, Vivien 43, 46-7, 63,
  92, *179*, 182
Durante, Viviana 23, 87, 90,
  186
  Romeo and Juliet 39, 172, *174*,
    176
Dyson, Paul 63

Edwards, Sian 102
Elektra 102
Ellis, David 21
English Heritage 159
English National Opera 46
Ensor, Dick 57, 157
Equity 26
European Union Health &
  Safety
    directives 180
    regulations 10
Evening Standard Awards 35, 39
Everitt, Anthony 71, 159
Eyre, Richard 66, 186
Eyre, Rosalind *37*, 171

La fanciulla del West 167, 170
Fanfare 38, 41
Fearful Symmetries 160, 168, 170
Fedora 144, 145-7
Fennell, Ron 30
Financial Times 74, 100
First Nights 22, 30, 34, 38, 184
Flies 11, 31
Floral Hall 157, 184
Flower, Jean 100, 102, 177
Flunkeys 64-5, 82, 90, 147-8,
  153
Follon, Andrew 112-13
Fonteyn, Dame Margot 11-12,
  49, 126
  feet & shoes 23, 86

The Force of Destiny 112
Forsythe, William 41, 168, 186
Freeman, Ron 78, 97, *165*
Freni, Mirella 8, 146, 148
Furtwängler, Gustav 12

Galas 46-47, 62-65, 106, 108,
  168
Gardiner, John Eliot 57
Garlick, Elaine 103-4, 123
Garrett, Eric 166
Gascoigne, Bamber 147, *179*,
  184
Gavron, Bob 66, *179*
Gawain 131, *132-3*, *135*, *136*,
  138
Gay, Bram *94*
Geraghty, Neil 176
Gheorghiu, Angela 8, 95, 148,
  186
Giordano, Umberto 145-7
Glasgow Theatre Royal 56
Glyndebourne 51
Gobbi, Tito 11-12
Government, national arts
  policy 59
Gowrie, Lord 138, 150, 159
Graham, Susan 95, 97, 100
Grahame, Shirley 75
Graves, Denyce 8, 77-8, 80,
  82-3, 86
  Carmen 81, 148
  Covent Garden Festival 148
Gray, Keith 117, 123, 130
Gray, Terri-Jayne 34, 80, 82-3,
  95
  Aida 153, 164
  Manon 166
  Die Meistersinger 32, 34
  Le nozze di Figaro 138-9
  Winter Gala 63, 65
Griffin, Bill 17
Guardian 35, 159
Guillem, Sylvie 8, 87, 168, 186
  Bolero 168
  Don Quixote 168
  Herman Schmerman 40, 41,
    64, 168
  Nureyev Gala 106
  Romeo and Juliet 108, 172
  Sissi 168
  Winter Gala 46
Gummer, Peter 91-2
Gurnett, Jane 100
Gustafson, Nancy 34

Haenchen, Hartmut 139
Haitink, Bernard 31-2, *55*, 105,
  177
  Der Ring des Nibelungen 185
  Die Meistersinger 32, 35
  Katya Kabanova 51

Hamlyn Week 80, 102
Hampton Court Palace Festival
  168
Hanson, Becky 117
Harrison, John 54, 147
Harsent, David 134
Hart, Matthew 38, 41, 104, 171
Hatley, Belinda 119
Hecklers *see* Stocken, Frederick
Henschel, Jane 185
Herman Schmerman 41, 64, 104,
  106, 168
Heseltine, Michael 150
Hilditch, Steve 155
Ho, Dr Stanley 42, 66, 70
Howells, Jonathan 104

If This Is Still A Problem 38-9,
  41, 87
In Focus study days 42
Independent 100, 170
industrial relations 65-6
Isaacs, Jeremy 8, *13*, *15*, 17, 31,
  35, 177
  BBC 14-15
  Carmen 82
  Covent Garden Festival 147-8
  criticism 47, 49
  development 12, 91-3
  finances 66, 183
  First Nights 105
  Joint Action Committee 157
  Katya Kabanova 50 54
  Le nozze di Figaro 139
  Manon 168
  Die Meistersinger 35
  Music Department 32
  Opera Board 19
  Phase II 159
  Stage Agreement 27
  unions 164
  Washington *120*, 130-1

Janáček, Leoš 8, 49, 54, 105-6
job security 14, 178
Johannsson, Kristjan 153
Joint Action Committee 70,
  91-3, 157, 178
Jones, Allen 127
Jones, Amanda 122, 127
Jones, Dame Gwyneth *167*, 170
Jones, Richard 185

Kalinina, Galina 153
Katona, Peter 95
Katya Kabanova 48, 49-51,
  52-3, 54-5, 93, 105-6,
  114-15
Keen, Terry *173*, 175
Kelly, Aileen 86, 103
Kennedy Center, Washington
  113, 117-18, 122

Kennedy, Sandy *70*, *144*
Key, Malcolm *182*

La Scala, Milan 50, 56, 78, 127,
  146
Labour Government 10
Lanchbery, John 88
Le Roux, François 134, *136*
Liszt, Franz 88
Lloyd-Webber, Andrew 47, 49,
  51
London City Ballet Gala 168
Lowe, Chris *179*
Lowery, Nigel 185
Lyceum Theatre 179
lyric theatres 9, 12

McDermott, Kevin 112
McDonald, Antony 95
McGorian, Elizabeth 113
McKenzie, Joan 176
Mackerras, Sir Charles 186
Mackerras, Judy 134
McMahon, Sir Kit 92, 155,
  157, 159, *179*
MacMillan, Deborah 108, *179*
MacMillan, Kenneth 19, 86,
  126
  Danses... 18
  Different Drummer 39
  Mayerling 87, 90
  Madama Butterfly 16-17, *28-9*
  The Magic Flute 56
Major, John 150
Makarova, Natalia 108
Manduell, Sir John *179*
Manon 127, 164, *165*, 166, 168
market-traders 14, 57
Markova, Dame Alicia 23
Marquis of Anglesey 157
Marsden, John 21, 134
Martinucci, Nicola *167*
Mason, Monica 171
Massenet, Jules 93, 100, 164
Maunder, Stuart 83, 166, 168
Mayerling 87, *89*, 90, 122, 172
Meade, Peter 62-3, 65, 146-8,
  186
Mehta, Zubin 12
Die Meistersinger von Nürnberg
  17-18, 31-2, *33*, 56, 93
  First Night 34-5
  Olivier Award 35
Metropolitan Opera House,
  New York 11, 126, 168, 170
Michael, Beth 22, 97, 151
Michaels-Moore, Anthony 166
Midland Bank Proms Week 102
Millennial Festivals 180
Millennium
  Commission 92, 184
  Fund 92, 160

Miller, Jonathan, *Così fan tutte* 186
Minkus, Léon 159
Les Misérables 17
Miss Piggy 108
Miss Saigon 178
Mitchell, Jane 22, 97, *101*, 151
Mitridate, rè di Ponto 35, 56
Monahan, Jim 57, 59, 157
Monahan, Judy 160
Morrice, Norman 19
Morris, Mike 66, 130-1
   BECTU 142-4, 148-9, 163-4, *163*
Morrissey, Gerry 143-4, 148-9, 162-3
Moshinsky, Elijah 152
Mosley, Philip 76
Mozart, Wolfgang Amadeus 8-9, 19, 186
   Le nozze di Figaro 93, 138-9
   Mitridate, rè di Ponto 35
   Die Zauberflöte 32, 55-6
Mukhamedov, Irek 8, 20, 87-8, 122, *158*
   American tour 119
   Fearful Symmetries 170
   Manon 127
   Nureyev Gala 108
   The Nutcracker 74
   Romeo and Juliet 39, 172, 176
Musicians' Union (MU) 26
Mustard Catering 47
Muti, Ricardo 78

National Heritage Fund 184
National Lottery 92, 160, 182-3
National Portrait Gallery 127
national touring 178
Naughtie, James 63-4
Nessun Dorma 186
New, George *183*, 184
New York Post 170
Nightgang 54, 143
Norman, Dame Jessye 78
Le nozze di Figaro 93, *137*, 138-9
Nunn, Michael 86-7, 119
Nunn, Trevor 8, 49-51, 54, 105
Nureyev Gala 106, 108
Nureyev, Rudolf 11-12, 106
The Nutcracker 20, 24, 26, 74, 76

Observer 56
Olivier Awards 35, 166
O'Neill, Dennis 153
opera, nature of 21-2
Opera House, Gothenburg 11
Opera North 17, 46
   General Administrator *see* Payne, Nicholas

Opera Studio 151
opéra-comique 77
Orchestra
   Age of Enlightenment 57
   Pit 12, 32, 38, 51, 95
      musicians 38
   Stalls 32
Ostrovsky, Aleksandr Nikolayevich 54, 105
Otello 175

Page, Ashley 104, *160*, 170-2
Palmer, Leana 123
Palmer, Vanessa 19, 123, 126
Palumbo, Lord 71, 91, 138, 159
Paris Opéra Ballet 8, 108, 168
Park, Dame Merle 24, 57, 171-2
Parrott, Andrew 56
Paul Hamlyn Foundation, sponsorship 80
Pavarotti, Luciano 8, 63, 151, 186
Payne, Nicholas 15, 19, 21, 56-7, 185
   Carmen 78
   Chérubin 95, 100
   Covent Garden Festival 147
   Gawain 131-4, 138
   Manon 168
   Die Meistersinger 35
   Music Department 32
   Le nozze di Figaro 93, 95
   Opera Board meetings 50-1, 93
   unions 164
   Die Zauberflöte 55-6
Peter Grimes 32
Peter Moores Foundation 42
Petipa, Marius 49, 159
The Phantom of the Opera 105
Piano Company Divertissements No 2 23
Porgy and Bess 51
Portillo, Michael 35
Potter, Beatrix 71
pregnancy 171
Price Waterhouse 26, 46
Priestley Report (1983) 159
Prince of Wales 46, 63
Princess Margaret 123, 130
Production
   Managers 50
   Workshops 30, 49
productions 18, 47
Prokina, Elena *52-3*
Prokofiev, Sergei 38-9, 172
Prompt Box 22, 51
public funding 9
Puccini, Giacomo 16-17, 20, 185
   La fanciulla del West 170

Turandot 186
Purcell, Henry 56

Rambert Dance Company 38
Rankl, Karl 77
Rautio, Nina 153
Ravel, Maurice 39
Reed, Adrian 38, 95, 97, 134
Reid, Dave 65, 117-18, 122
Renard 104, 170
Rencher, Derek 113, 117, 171
Renwick, Sir Robin *120*
resident companies 17
Das Rheingold 185-6
Ricciarelli, Katia 151
Rigoletto 102
Der Ring des Nibelungen 66, 185
Roberts, Nicola 171-2
Robertson, Allen 39
Romeo and Juliet 37, 38-9, 172, *175*, 176
Ronson, Gail 43, 47
Roocroft, Amanda 56, 186
Rossini, Gioachino 8, 185-6
   Mosè in Egitto 102
roster shift system 27
The Royal Ballet 8, 17, 20, 119, 122, 126
   Administrative Director *see* Russell-Roberts, Anthony
   American tour 49, 86, 126, 142, 170
   Assistant Director *see* Mason, Monica
   Corps de Ballet 20, 35, 38, 126
      First Artist 19
   Director *see* Dowell, Anthony; Morrice, Norman
   founder 175
   mini-tour 103, 170
   move 159
   Music Director 38, 88
   preparation 22
   Press Officer 122, 127
   Principals 20-21, 64, 87
   productions 9, 18, 127
   purpose-built home 57
   School
      children 24, 26, 74-6
      Director *see* Park, Dame Merle
      Lower School 20, 23
      Upper School 20, 23, 119
   royal charter 23
The Royal Opera
   Artistic Administrator *see* Katona, Peter
   Associate Music Director *see* Downes, Sir Edward
   Director *see* Payne, Nicholas

Music
   Department staff 32
   Director *see* Haitink, Bernard
   Head *see* Syrus, David
   Opera Chorus 21-2, 56, 151
      Chorus Master 80
   Opera Company 49, 170
      Manager *see* Gray, Terri-Jayne
   productions 9
Royal Opera House, The 17
   Assistant Technical Director *see* Seekings, John
   ballet, resident company 23
   Ballet Rest Area 175-6
   Boards
      Ballet Board 19, 43
         Chairman *see* Blackstone, Baroness Tessa
      Birmingham Royal Ballet Board 19
      Development Board 19, 57
         Chairman *see* McMahon, Sir Kit
      Main Board 19, 43, 49-50, 182
         Chairman *see* Stirling, Sir Angus
      meetings 9, 12
      Opera Board 19, 50, 93
         Chairman *see* Spooner, Sir James
      reports 180
   budget (1994/95) 66
   Chief Electrician *see* Watson, Paul
   development 47, 57, 91
      closure 177-80
      Phase I 11
      Phase II 12, 57, 59, 93, 155
      programme 155, 159
      refurbishment 10
      relocation 178-80, 182
      reopening 12
      return 178
      site 10, 147, 155
         development costs 182
      team 157
   Development Land Trust 10-11
   Development Project 155
      Chief Executive *see* Ensor, Dick
   Director of Administration *see* Wright, Richard
   Director of Corporate/Public Affairs & Marketing *see* Cooper, Keith
   Education Department 183
   Finance
      Committee 47

(Royal Opera House, The Finance cont.)
Department 19
Finance Director *see* Timms, Clive
finances 9, 26, 159
freehold 11
General Director *see* Isaacs, Jeremy
Marketing Manager *see* Temple, Ian
Merchandising Manager *see* McDermott, Kevin
Personnel Director 31, 65-6
Personnel Manager *see* Vickers, Judith
Press Officer *see* Anderson, Helen
Public Appeal 182
shop 112
Staff Restaurant 87
Technical Director *see* Harrison, John
touring costs 178
Trust 42-43, 46
Annual Lunch 43, 46
Chairman *see* Butler, Jim
Deputy Chairman *see* Duffield, Vivien
Director *see* Clark, Felicity
Royal Shakespeare Company 8, 54, 159
Rozhdestvensky, Gennadi 95, 97, 100, 112
Russell-Roberts, Anthony 19, 49-50, 130

Sabbatini, Giuseppe *165*
Sadler, Richard 80
Sadler's Wells
Ballet 23
theatre 179-80
Sainsbury, Lord 92, 182
Saunders, Christopher 119, 172
Schaaf, Johannes 138
schedules 18, 34
Schenk, Otto 106
Schoenberg, Arnold 39
Scottish Opera 55
security 127, 130
Seekings, John 65, 117-18, 122, 142, 144
workforce negotiations 149
Shicoff, Neil 78, 82
Sibley, Antoinette 19, 39
Siegfried 185
Sikora, Elizabeth 54
singers 8, 21, 82, 150
sitzprobe 22
The Sleeping Beauty 47, 49, 113, 117, 122-3, 186, *see also*

American tour
Bjørnson, Maria 47, 49-50, 113, *116*, 117, 130
Bussell, Darcey *110-11*, *116*, *124-5*, 126-7, 130
Chadwick, Fiona 172
Dowell, Anthony 113, 117, 127, *128-9*, 130
Solymosi, Zoltán *124-5*, 130
Solti, Sir Georg 12, 32, 186
Solymosi, Zoltán 87-8, *89*, 127
Nureyev Gala 108
The Sleeping Beauty 124-5, 130
The Nutcracker 20
South Bank 92
Spectator 106, 153
Spencer, Charles 27, 30
Spencer, Nicki 146
Spooner, Sir James 47, 50, 93
Stage 12, 95
Agreement 27, 164
crew 30, 103
dancers 38
Door 30, 62, 155
Head Keeper 62-3, 65
machinery 11
Managers 22, 34, 97
Rehearsals 22
time 19
stagehands 22
Stanhope Properties 93
Stevenson, Margaret 177
Stirling, Sir Angus 9, 14-15, 93, *see also* Arts Council; *Winter Gala*
Price Waterhouse report 26
Stocken, Frederick 138
The Storm 54, 105
Strauss, Richard 102
Stravinsky, Igor 104
Studer, Cheryl 152-3
Styles, Pat 143
Sunday Telegraph 168
Sunday Times 56, 138
Sunday working 164
Sunset Boulevard 51, 54
Sweet, Sharon 153
Sydney Opera 102
Sylvester, Michael 153
Syrus, David 32, 51, 134, 166, 168

Tales of Beatrix Potter 9, *68-9*, 74, 171
American tour 122
double bill 20
Tallis, Jacqui 176
Tate Gallery 92
Tate, Jeffrey 83
Tatler 127
Tchaikovsky, Pytor Ilich 19, 64,

126, 186, *see also The Nutcracker; Winter Gala*
Te Kanawa, Dame Kiri 8, 21, 46, 105
Winter Gala 61, 64
Teatro Comunale, Bologna 56
Temple, Ian 74
Terfel, Bryn 8, *137*, 138, 186
Theatre Royal, Drury Lane 178
Theatres Trust 179
three-day week 27, 30
tickets 42, 71, 74
Time Out 39
The Times 100, 168
Timms, Clive 66, 91, 131
timpanists, Nigel & Ronnie 34
Tippett, Sir Michael 39
Tomlinson, John 34-5, 134, *135*, 138, 185
Tooley, John 17, 30-1
Torini, Peter 16-17
Tosca 20, 146
training courses 30
Tranah, Nicola *156*
La traviata 66, 186
Trent, Matthew 176
Tuckett, William 65, 88, 171
Desirable Hostilities 104
Is This Still.. 38-9, 41, 87
Tuckey, Andrew *179*
Turandot 186

unions 26, 31

Vaduva, Leontina 164, 166
de Valois, Dame Ninette 23, 172, 175
studio 42
Van Allan, Richard 166
Varady, Julia 153
Verdi 8, 19
Aida 9, 150-3
The Force of Destiny 112
Otello 175
Rigoletto 102
Un ballo in maschera 106, 153
Versace, Gianni 41
Vic-Wells company 23
Vick, Graham 32, 35, 56, 147
Vickers, Jon 32
Vickers, Judith 66, 142-3
workforce negotiations 149
Vienna State Opera 56, 102
von Otter, Anne Sofie 186
De Vos, Ann *160*

Wagner, Richard 8, 31, 153, 185-6
orchestra 17
Waldman, Michael 14, 24, *120*, 130
interviews

Arnold, Ivell 154-5
Chadwick, Fiona 176
Duffield, Vivien 63
Graves, Denyce 78
Hart, Matthew 38
Michael, Beth 151
Monahan, Jim 59
Die Walküre 185-6
wardrobe 30, 49
Warnock
Dame Mary 9
Report (1992) 26, 46, 56, 70
Watson, Paul 117, 142
Webern, Arnold 39
Webster, David 17
Webster, Sir John 31
Welsh National Opera 19, 178
Wembley Arena 42
Wembley opera 152
Westminster City Council 12, 47, 57, 59
Phase II 155, 157, 159
sponsorship 80
Wheel, Geoff 50
Wheen, Natalie 41
White Hot and Different 39, 47, 57
White Lodge *see* The Royal Ballet, Lower School
Wicks, Stephen 176
Wildor, Sarah 172
Willems, Thom 41
Winbergh, Gøsta 34
Wings 11-12, 64
Winter Dreams 39, *158*, 168
Winter Gala 46-7, *60*, *61*, 62-5, 106, 168
Wordsworth, Barry 38, 88
world wars 10
First, submarine engine 11
Second 23
Wright, Richard 30-1, 65-6, 149
Wright, Sir Peter 75

Yeargan, Michael 152
Young, Simone 102

Die Zauberflöte 32, 42, *44-5*, 55-6